Philippians
Colossians &
Philemon

Philippians Colossians & Philemon

DAVID E. WALKER

CONTENTS

PREFACE

This commentary originated from the teaching ministry the Lord has given me at the church I pastor. I first taught these books of the Bible verse by verse, in either our Sunday school or Wednesday night classes. As I prepared my lessons, I decided to write them in commentary form for publishing.

This commentary is unique in the following ways.

First, it makes no attempt to correct, revise, or alter the King James text in *any* fashion. I write from the perspective of accepting the Authorized King James Bible as the inspired word of God without error (2 Tim. 3:15-16). Consequently, you will not be given examples from the Hebrew or Greek where the King James text could be clarified.

Next, this commentary is written from a dispensational approach to theology as opposed to the reformed Calvinistic position. The Bible will be presented in the literal sense and proper divisions regarding God's covenants and dispensations will be highlighted.

Along the lines of practicality, this series strives to speak as much to the heart as to the head. The Bible was not given merely to fill our heads with more facts, but to fill our hearts with more love for the Saviour. An attempt to emphasize good, sensible, and useful truths is a main objective in this commentary.

I have included a few expository outlines in this series. But, since "every word of God is pure" (Prov. 30:5), the layout will be based on a verse-by-verse structure rather than an expository or outline style. I have endeavored to comment on each verse as it relates in its proper context, while stressing doctrinal and practical meanings.

Finally, I have written this commentary from the standpoint of an independent Baptist pastor who is simply a student of the scriptures. Hopefully, the content will glorify Jesus Christ, while coming across simple, plain, and straightforward.

I pray that you might be blessed from studying the Bible alongside of this commentary.

PHILIPPIANS

INTRODUCTION

The book of Philippians was written by the apostle Paul around AD 62-64 during his imprisonment in Rome (mentioned in Acts 28). It contains 4 chapters, 104 verses and 2,183 words (Vance, 218).

Philippi (named after Philip of Macedonia who was the father of Alexander the Great) means "a lover of horses." Predominately Gentile, it was a Roman military colony in Macedonia about nine miles from the Aegean Sea. No Jewish synagogues were at Philippi.

During Paul's second missionary journey, he and Silas became acquainted with Philippi. After the Lord forbade them to go north or east, Paul had a vision of a Macedonian man saying, "Come over into Macedonia, and help us" (Acts 16:9); so, they left Troas and went west to Philippi.

On the Sabbath day, he and Silas went out of the city "by a river side" where other Christians went to pray. A woman named Lydia was there, and she became their first convert. From this initial contact, the church of Philippi was established.

However, not everyone at Philippi was pleased. Paul and Silas were arrested and put in jail for preaching the gospel. But as they sang praises to the Lord, there was an earthquake, and all the prisoners were suddenly loosed. The jailor was so affected by the testimony of Paul and Silas, that he was saved, along with his household (Acts 16:26-34).

After Paul left Philippi, the church still ministered to his needs, but when he was imprisoned in Rome, they lost contact with him for a few years. When they finally found out where he was, they sent Epaphroditus with an offering.

Paul wrote his letter to the Philippians from the Roman prison and sent it by the hand of Epaphroditus. He did not write this letter to correct their doctrine (like he did with the Galatians), nor did he reprove them for bad conduct (like he did with the Corinthians). The only problem Paul mentioned was a minor disagreement between two women (Phil. 4:2).

The theme of Philippians is the Christian experience. It is a practical book about the heart of true Christian devotion, teaching that joy is not found in circumstances but rather in Jesus Christ. The key words are **"joy"** (occurring six times) and **"rejoice"** (occurring ten times). Paul wrote about his joy when he was in prison and suffering for Christ. There, while suffering, **"rejoice with me"** (Phil. 2:18), even though they would be called upon to **"suffer for his sake"** (Phil. 1:29).

In addition to his practical teaching, Paul also affirmed several doctrines in the book: eternal security (1:6); the Christian's life after death (1:20-23); the deity of Christ (1:6-11); the righteousness of God (3:9); the perfection of the believer (3:11-15); the rapture (3:20, 21); rewards for service (3:1); answers to prayer (4:6,7); and giving and receiving (4:14-15).

The book can be outlined as: Chapter 1 – the single mind; Chapter 2 – the submissive mind; Chapter 3 – the spiritual mind and Chapter 4 – the secure mind (Wiersbe, 63).

PHILIPPIANS CHAPTER 1

---

1 Paul and Timotheus, the servants of Jesus Christ, to all the saints in Christ Jesus which are at Philippi, with the bishops and deacons:

Paul opened his letter to the Philippians by introducing Timothy in the salutation. While we understand that Paul is the human author, he still included his young protégée in the greeting. Timothy had probably been visiting him in Rome at that time, and Paul had planned to send Timothy to check on the Philippians' spiritual welfare (see Phil. 2:19).

"To all the saints…" Paul addressed this letter to three groups: the saints, the bishops and the deacons. The **"saints"** are, of course, *living* Christians. The idea that saints are dead heroes to whom we can pray to is an unbiblical Roman Catholic fabrication. While **"saints"** can refer to angels (Deut 32:2, 3; Dan. 8:13; Jude 14 with 2 Thess. 1:7 and Matt. 24:31) in Paul's epistles they generally refer to *living* believers.

"With the bishops…" The **"bishops"** were the leaders of the church, what we today call *pastors*. The word "bishop" means to be an "overseer" and is also used interchangeably with the word "elder" (Titus 1:5-7). We call elders *pastors* because both Paul and Peter commanded the elders to "feed the church of God" (Acts 20:28)…"feed the flock of God which is among you" (1 Peter 5:1-2).

"And deacons." In the early church, Christians were expected to sell their possessions and pool their resources (Acts 2:44-45). The church was also responsible for widows who didn't have a means of support. Unlike modern America, Jerusalem in the first century had no social security or disability programs. So, when the congregation grew to about eight thousand (Acts 2:41, 4:4) the Lord directed them to choose deacons to help with these matters. The word "deacon" literally means "runners through the dust" (Dr. Ruckman, 362).

These men had to be "of honest report, full of the Holy Ghost and wisdom" (Acts 6:3) and "grave, not doubletongued, not given to much wine, not greedy of filthy lucre" (1 Tim 3:8). Their wives were also to be "grave, not slanderers, sober, faithful in all things" (1 Tim. 3:11). These qualifications were necessary for those helping with personal problems, dealing with family situations, and receiving money from donations. The scriptures also outline which widows were to be accepted in the program (1 Tim. 5:3-6).

---

2 Grace *be* unto you, and peace, from God our Father, and *from* the Lord Jesus Christ.

Notice that Paul's salutation included a greeting from the Lord, confirming not only the dual authorship of scripture (human and divine) but also its inspiration. This letter is from **"God our Father, and from the Lord Jesus Christ"** as well as from Paul and Timothy.

---

3 I thank my God upon every remembrance of you,
4 Always in every prayer of mine for you all making request with joy,
5 For your fellowship in the gospel from the first day until now;

Paul was thankful when he thought about the church at Philippi. He had no reason to be upset or flustered because they were a good church that had been good to him.

Notice the key word **"joy"** in verse four. The theme of *joy* runs through this epistle. Every time Paul prayed for them; he had joy in his heart.

"For your fellowship in the gospel..." has to do with how the church at Philippi ministered to Paul's needs. They supported him in the work that he was doing for God; this was part of their fellowship. Likewise, when we support missions, we have a part in those ministries. Even though we may never set foot on mission soil, we can have **"fellowship in the gospel"** by supporting those whom God calls.

---

6 Being confident of this very thing, that he which hath begun a good work in you will perform *it* until the day of Jesus Christ:

Practically speaking, Paul encouraged the Philippians to *not quit* in their Christian journey. In other words, when God begins something, He will finish it. Don't quit! While you might not see all the rewards *now*, you *will* eventually.

> And let us not be weary in well doing: for in due season we shall reap, if we faint not. (Gal. 6:9)

> Therefore, my beloved brethren, be ye stedfast, unmoveable, always abounding in the work of the Lord, forasmuch as ye know that your labour is not in vain in the Lord. (1 Cor. 15:58)

Doctrinally, this verse also supports eternal security. God is the One who saved you and started this *new* **"work"** in you, and He will finish it! It is God's salvation to finish, not yours! Paul says later that "it is God which worketh in you" (Phil. 2:13).

The **"day of Jesus Christ"** is primarily a reference to the rapture and the judgment seat of Christ. Note the following references: 1 Cor. 1:7-

8; 1 Cor. 3:11-15; 1 Cor. 5:4-5; 2 Cor. 1:14; 1 Thess. 2:19; Phil. 1:10, 2:16; and 2 Tim. 1:12, 18.

Our confidence is not in our works or ability to perform, but rather in God's ability to keep us until the Lord returns to take us to glory.

---

7 Even as it is meet for me to think this of you all, because I have you in my heart; inasmuch as both in my bonds, and in the defence and confirmation of the gospel, ye all are partakers of my grace.

8 For God is my record, how greatly I long after you all in the bowels of Jesus Christ.

"Even as it is meet..." To be **"meet"** means that something is proper, that it "matches." In other words, it was fitting for Paul to be thinking of them because of their unique fellowship. Paul was so close to them that it was as if they were in bonds with him. He also rejoiced that they were defending him, knowing that they stood behind him in his effort.

In verse eight, when he mentions the **"bowels of Jesus Christ,"** he is referring to the inner feelings that he had for them. Webster's 1828 dictionary defines "bowels" as "the interior part of any thing; as the bowels of the earth."

---

9 And this I pray, that your love may abound yet more and more in knowledge and *in* all judgment;

10 That ye may approve things that are excellent; that ye may be sincere and without offence till the day of Christ;

11 Being filled with the fruits of righteousness, which are by Jesus Christ, unto the glory and praise of God.

Paul's longing was not just to see the Philippians but also to access their spiritual welfare. In verses 9-11 we have a five-fold prayer request, maybe the previous **"request"** from verse four:

1. That **"your love may abound yet more and more."**
2. That **"ye may approve things that are excellent."**
3. That **"ye may be sincere."**
4. That **"ye may be...without offence."**
5. That ye be **"filled with the fruits of righteousness."**

The abounding of their love was to be according to **"knowledge and in all judgment."** We are not to have the blind love of indiscriminate tolerance, like as commonly promoted by modern America. Christians must use sound judgment about what they should or shouldn't love. An easy rule of thumb is to love what God loves and hate what God hates. To have this **"knowledge"** you must read the scriptures, which reveal the mind and heart of God. They tell us what God loves and what He hates (see Prov. 6:16-19).

The next request **("approve things that are excellent")** is for the Christian to use his God given ability to make judgments. Contrary to popular consensus, Christians are commanded to judge:

> But he that is spiritual judgeth all things, yet he himself is judged of no man. (1 Cor. 2:15)

> Do ye not know that the saints shall judge the world? and if the world shall be judged by you, are ye unworthy to judge the smallest matters? Know ye not that we shall judge angels? how much more things that pertain to this life? (1 Cor. 6:2-3)

Christians are to judge according to the word of God. We are to "prove it!" "Prove all things; hold fast that which is good" (1 Thess. 5:21). The Bible is the standard we use. If something does not line up with the scriptures, it is wrong. It is as simple as that.

Request numbers three and four are about Christian conduct. Paul wanted them to be **"sincere and without offence."** This does *not* mean a Christian can live a sinless life, but it *does* mean we should be honest and above reproach. A good example are the lives of the parents of John the Baptist and the apostle Paul:

> And they were both righteous before God, walking in all the commandments and ordinances of the Lord blameless. (Luke 1:6)

> And herein do I exercise myself, to have always a conscience void of offence toward God, and toward men. (Acts 24:16)

The last request in Paul's prayer concerns bearing fruit for Jesus Christ. In John 15:8 Jesus said the Father is glorified when we "bear much fruit." Here the request is that we be **"filled with the fruits of righteousness."** The only way for this to happen is **"by Jesus Christ"** bearing fruit inside of us. As believer's we must allow Jesus Christ to have control, so we can be "filled with the Spirit" (Eph. 5:18).

---

12 But I would ye should understand, brethren, that the things *which happened* unto me have fallen out rather unto the furtherance of the gospel;
13 So that my bonds in Christ are manifest in all the palace, and in all other *places*;
14 And many of the brethren in the Lord, waxing confident by my bonds, are much more bold to speak the word without fear.
15 Some indeed preach Christ even of envy and strife; and some also of good will:
16 The one preach Christ of contention, not sincerely, supposing to add affliction to my bonds:
17 But the other of love, knowing that I am set for the defence of the gospel.
18 What then? notwithstanding, every way, whether in pretence, or in truth, Christ is preached; and I therein do rejoice, yea, and will rejoice.

When Paul explained the situation of his being in jail, his entire tone was one of rejoicing and contentment. He first stated that the gospel was spreading further than it had prior to his being imprisoned (verse twelve). The **"palace"** and other **"places"** were hearing the gospel because of Paul's misfortune.

Not only was the gospel spreading, but some of the **"brethren"** were **"much more bold to speak the word without fear"** (verse fourteen). Paul's incarceration lit a fire in the hearts of young preachers and gave them confidence to preach about Christ. When they thought of Paul's circumstances, and his faithfulness, they took courage that they could continue as well. After all, they were free, not behind bars. What was stopping them from preaching?

"Some…preach Christ even of envy and strife…" Some people mentioned the name of Christ in a derogatory way or with a negative context, but their words didn't bother Paul. He rejoiced that Christ's name was being spoken and that people were seeing that the movement (which was spoken against – Acts 28:22) had power behind it.

---

19 For I know that this shall turn to my salvation through your prayer, and the supply of the Spirit of Jesus Christ,

---

Here the word **"salvation"** is used in the physical sense of the body as in these other verses:

Take heed unto thyself, and unto the doctrine; continue in them: for in doing this thou shalt both save thyself, and them that hear thee. (1 Tim. 4:16)

Notwithstanding she shall be saved in childbearing, if they continue in faith and charity and holiness with sobriety. (1 Tim. 2:15)

And the prayer of faith shall save the sick, and the Lord shall raise him up; and if he have committed sins, they shall be forgiven him. (James 5:15)

Let him know, that he which converteth the sinner from the error of his way shall save a soul from death, and shall hide a multitude of sins. (James 5:20)

Paul was confident that their prayers would deliver him from prison (compare with 2 Tim. 4:17-18).

"The supply of the Spirit of Jesus Christ" has to do with their prayers of "supplication" (Phil. 4:6). The supplies that Paul needed were greater than physical needs. He needed the Spirit of the Lord to strengthen him.

---

20 According to my earnest expectation and *my* hope, that in nothing I shall be ashamed, but *that* with all boldness, as always, so now also Christ shall be magnified in my body, whether *it be* by life, or by death.

21 For to me to live *is* Christ, and to die *is* gain.

22 But if I live in the flesh, this *is* the fruit of my labour: yet what I shall choose I wot not.

23 For I am in a strait betwixt two, having a desire to depart, and to be with Christ; which is far better:

24 Nevertheless to abide in the flesh *is* more needful for you.

"Nothing I shall be ashamed..." Paul was not ashamed of being in prison nor of the reproach that accompanied taking up his cross and following the Lord. Neither was he "ashamed of the gospel of Christ" (Rom. 1:20). In 2 Timothy Paul also exhorted Timothy not to be ashamed of the Lord or of him:

> Be not thou therefore ashamed of the testimony of our Lord, nor of me his prisoner: but be thou partaker of the afflictions of the gospel according to the power of God. (2 Tim 1:8)

As a Christian you have no reason to be apologetic or embarrassed for what you believe. You should stand tall and be bold for Jesus Christ. Boldness is an indication of closeness with the Lord:

Now when they saw the boldness of Peter and John, and perceived that they were unlearned and ignorant men, they marvelled; and they took knowledge of them, that they had been with Jesus. (Acts 4:13)

"Christ shall be magnified in my body..." Hence, we are commanded to present our "bodies a living sacrifice" (Rom. 12:1). Jesus Christ is to be lifted up and magnified *in us,* so we must yield to the Spirit of God instead of to the flesh:

Neither yield ye your members as instruments of unrighteousness unto sin: but yield yourselves unto God, as those that are alive from the dead, and your members as instruments of righteousness unto God. (Rom. 6:13)

For ye are bought with a price: therefore glorify God in your body, and in your spirit, which are God's. (1 Cor. 6:20)

"Whether it be by life, or by death." John the Baptist epitomized this verse. He said, "He must increase, but I must decrease" (John 3:30), and he actually decreased to the extent that he lost his head (Mark 6:24-25).

Sadly, Christians today would rather live themselves and let Jesus hang dead on the cross because they don't want to die or be dethroned. The Bible teaches us that we are to be **"crucified with Christ"** (Gal. 2:20), so the life of Jesus Christ can live in us.

Paul's attitude was one of a *servant.* He wanted to be obedient and willing to do whatever was necessary for Christ to be magnified. If it was by his life of imprisonment or by his death, he was content as long as Jesus Christ got the preeminence.

"For to me to live is Christ..." In other words, Jesus Christ was everything to the apostle Paul. When he wasn't preaching about Jesus Christ, he was praying to Him. When he wasn't praying to Him, he was writing about Him. When he wasn't writing about Him, he was thinking about Him. Jesus Christ filled Paul's heart and mind, and so should He fill our hearts and minds.

American Christians allow so many other things to be "life" to them, when "life" should be centered around the person of the Lord Jesus Christ. Whenever we fail to give Jesus the proper place, life and its meaning become imbalanced.

"And to die is gain." This is where we get the saying for a Christian after death: "He's a lot better off now." Indeed, any Christian is "better off" after death. And here, Paul tells us that death is a **"gain."** This verse, along with verse twenty-three, teaches that at death a Christian goes immediately to be with Jesus Christ. The idea of "soul sleep," espoused by the Jehovah's Witnesses, is completely unbiblical. If at death you simply went in the grave to sleep, what would be the gain? Below are other scriptures that verify where the soul of a Christian goes at death:

We are confident, I say, and willing rather to be absent from the body, and to be present with the Lord. (2 Cor. 5:8)

For if we believe that Jesus died and rose again, even so them also which sleep in Jesus will God bring with him. (1 Thess. 4:14)

And there came thither certain Jews from Antioch and Iconium, who persuaded the people, and, having stoned Paul, drew him out of the city, supposing he had been dead. (Acts 14:19)

I knew a man in Christ above fourteen years ago, (whether in the body, I cannot tell; or whether out of the body, I cannot tell: God knoweth;) such an one caught up to the third heaven. (2 Cor. 12:2)

"Strait betwixt two…" Paul contemplated which he would rather have, if God allowed the choice. Would he rather stay on earth and let Christ be magnified in his body, or would he rather go to the chopping block and depart to the third heaven before his head hit the ground? Let us not forget that Paul had already seen glory (see the verses above) and had *tasted* heaven.

The only thing, besides the will of God, that motivated Paul to keep living was the need of the churches **("to abide in the flesh is more needful for you").** He had a genuine concern for their spiritual well-being (see also 2 Cor. 11:28).

---

25 And having this confidence, I know that I shall abide and continue with you all for your furtherance and joy of faith;

26 That your rejoicing may be more abundant in Jesus Christ for me by my coming to you again.

Paul was confident that it was the will of God for him to keep living, so he could continue to minister to the churches. He then alluded to his getting out of prison (verse twenty-six), which would bring great **"rejoicing"** from the Philippians. If he did indeed get out of prison, this would indicate that Paul had two imprisonments (Acts 28 and 2 Tim. 4).

---

27 Only let your conversation be as it becometh the gospel of Christ: that whether I come and see you, or else be absent, I may hear of your affairs, that ye stand fast in one spirit, with one mind striving together for the faith of the gospel;

The word **"conversation"** means conduct and manner of life, rather than just speech.

For ye have heard of my conversation in time past in the Jews' religion, how that beyond measure I persecuted the church of God, and wasted it. (Gal. 1:13)

Among whom also we all had our conversation in times past in the lusts of our flesh, fulfilling the desires of the flesh and of the mind; and were by nature the children of wrath, even as others. (Eph. 2:3)

That ye put off concerning the former conversation the old man, which is corrupt according to the deceitful lusts. (Eph. 4:22)

For our conversation is in heaven; from whence also we look for the Saviour, the Lord Jesus Christ. (Phil. 3:20)

Let no man despise thy youth; but be thou an example of the believers, in word, in conversation, in charity, in spirit, in faith, in purity. (1 Tim. 4:12)

Likewise, ye wives, be in subjection to your own husbands; that, if any obey not the word, they also may without the word be won by the conversation of the wives; While they behold your chaste conversation coupled with fear. (1 Peter 3:1-2

"As it becometh the gospel of Christ..." This verse also concerns Christian conduct and teaches us that **"the gospel of Christ"** entails more than just the death, burial, and resurrection of our Lord. It has to do with how Christians represent the Lord as **"ambassadors"** (2 Cor. 5:20). If we live like the world and allow the flesh to control us, then we could "hinder the gospel of Christ" (1 Cor. 9:12). In 2 Corinthians Paul also connects Christian stewardship (giving) with subjection to the gospel:

Whiles by the experiment of this ministration they glorify God for your professed subjection unto the gospel of Christ, and for your liberal distribution unto them, and unto all men. (2 Cor. 9:13)

"Stand fast..." We know what it means to *stand*. And the word **"fast"** does *not* refer to quickly, but rather, to something being "firm" like a "fastener." **"Stand fast"** means "a firm, fixed, or settled position" (Webster). It is related to militaristic defense:

Declare ye in Egypt, and publish in Migdol, and publish in Noph and in Tahpanhes: say ye, Stand fast, and prepare thee; for the sword shall devour round about thee. (Jer. 46:14)

Watch ye, stand fast in the faith, quit you like men, be strong. (1 Cor. 16:13)

Paul did not want to hear that they had digressed in position or apostatized ("falling from a standing position"). Therefore, Paul is exhorting them to *stand,* much like he encouraged the Ephesians:

Put on the whole armour of God, that ye may be able to <u>stand</u> against the wiles of the devil. For we wrestle not against flesh and blood, but against principalities, against powers, against the rulers of the darkness of this world, against spiritual wickedness in high places. Wherefore take unto you the whole armour of God, that ye may be able to withstand in the evil day, and having done all, to stand. Stand therefore, having your loins girt about with truth, and having on the breastplate of righteousness. (Eph. 6:11-14)

"One mind striving together..." This is true Christian unity. We are told "to keep the unity of the Spirit" (Eph. 4:3), but not at the expense of truth or doctrine. In studying the life of Jesus Christ and the apostles, you will find that they often caused *division.* The way we keep unity is to keep our doctrine and motives pure and our fellowship centered around Jesus Christ. Compromise of either motives or doctrine will destroy biblical unity.

---

28 And in nothing terrified by your adversaries: which is to them an evident token of perdition, but to you of salvation, and that of God.

Paul didn't want the Philippians to fear those who were threatening them. The justice and judgment of God would see that their detractors would get what they deserved. **"Perdition"** refers to "destruction" and judgment:

Seeing it is a righteous thing with God to recompense tribulation to them that trouble you. (2 Thess. 1:6)

Their persecution was also a verification that they were saved, and that God was for them. Throughout the Bible, God's people have been persecuted. Jesus said to the disciples, "If they have persecuted me, they will also persecute you" (John 15:20).

---

29 For unto you it is given in the behalf of Christ, not only to believe on him, but also to suffer for his sake;
30 Having the same conflict which ye saw in me, and now hear *to be* in me.

Notice that suffering as a Christian is said to be a *gift* from the Lord. New Testament Christians suffered persecution and even rejoiced during their persecution.

> That no man should be moved by these afflictions: for yourselves know that we are appointed thereunto. (1 Thess. 3:3)

> For even hereunto were ye called: because Christ also suffered for us, leaving us an example, that ye should follow his steps. (1 Peter 2:21)

> And to him they agreed: and when they had called the apostles, and beaten them, they commanded that they should not speak in the name of Jesus, and let them go. And they departed from the presence of the council, rejoicing that they were counted worthy to suffer shame for his name. And daily in the temple, and in every house, they ceased not to teach and preach Jesus Christ. (Acts 5:40-42)

Paul desired to be more acquainted with "the fellowship of [Christ's] sufferings" (Phil. 3:10). We wonder why the church of today has lost its power, but I think the answer is in the fact that we don't have to suffer. There must be a crucifixion before a death, and a death before a resurrection. We want resurrection power with only Gethsemane submission. And it simply does not work that way.

"The same conflict..." relates to Paul being in jail for his faith. In this first chapter Paul encouraged the Philippians to keep their fire burning for God, despite his imprisonment, or their future persecution. The strength to keep living for God is *joy* (Neh. 8:10).

Philippians Chapter 2

---

1 If *there be* therefore any consolation in Christ, if any comfort of love, if any fellowship of the Spirit, if any bowels and mercies,

2 Fulfil ye my joy, that ye be likeminded, having the same love, *being* of one accord, of one mind.

Paul begins chapter two with four conditional **"if"** clauses that imply the conditions have *already* been met. In other words, "Since there is consolation, since there is comfort of love…fulfill ye my joy."

"Consolation in Christ" has to do with the comfort that is given to us as believers. Paul expounds upon this comfort in 2 Cor. 1:5-7.

"Comfort of love" comes from knowing that we are loved by God – something that unsaved people have never experienced.

> And hope maketh not ashamed; because the love of God is shed abroad in our hearts by the Holy Ghost which is given unto us. (Rom. 5:5)

Then Paul mentions the **"fellowship of the Spirit."** We have fellowship with the Spirit because the Spirit dwells in our bodies (1 Cor. 6:19). Furthermore, we commune with the Spirit through prayer and acknowledgment of our position in Christ:

> And because ye are sons, God hath sent forth the Spirit of his Son into your hearts, crying, Abba, Father. (Gal. 4:6)

"Bowels and mercies" have to do with the inner feelings of Jesus Christ and the attitude of the Lord toward us. Compare this phrase with Phil. 1:8. Remember when Moses wanted to see God? God told Moses that he could not see His face, but that He would pass by him. When God passed by, He made a proclamation about Himself, which was God's theology lesson to Moses. Notice that the first attribute the Lord records is *mercy*.

> And the LORD passed by before him, and proclaimed, The LORD, The LORD God, merciful and gracious, longsuffering, and abundant in goodness and truth. (Ex. 34:6)

While grace is God giving you what you *don't* deserve, mercy is God not giving you what you *do* deserve. Aren't you thankful that the Lord is merciful?

So, in light of verse one, Paul is getting pragmatic again, exhorting the Philippians to **"be likeminded...being of one accord, of one mind."** And by heeding that exhortation, they would be fulfilling Paul's joy.

The subject of unity is again touched upon (verse two). But this time Paul is going to explain how we can have unity through the right attitude or **"mind."**

---

3 Let nothing *be done* through strife or vainglory; but in lowliness of mind let each esteem other better than themselves.

4 Look not every man on his own things, but every man also on the things of others.

If verse three were only obeyed, we could avoid so many problems in our families, workplaces, and churches. **"Strife"** has to do with getting revenge, and **"vainglory"** is connected with self acclamation. Both are siblings of *pride* and opposite to **"lowliness of mind."** The following verses are great commentaries:

> With all lowliness and meekness, with longsuffering, forbearing one another in love. (Eph. 4:2)

> Be kindly affectioned one to another with brotherly love; in honour preferring one another. (Rom. 12:10)

Do you really think better of others than you do of yourself? Humility is not just a presence but an attitude. The person who thinks about himself all of the time is *not* humble. We get closer to this New Testament command when we cease thinking of ourselves.

The next time you hear something negative about a fellow Christian and begin to compare yourself with him, stop and ask yourself the following questions:

1. Am I being fair in my judgment?
2. What would the Lord think of my condescending attitude toward this person?
3. If my inner thoughts were known, would others think the same of me?
4. Am I praying for this person as much as I am condemning him?

Verse four brings verse three into perspective. Looking **"on the things of others"** carries with it the idea of true concern, which is a by-product of real humility. In other words, we shouldn't be so engrossed in our own lives and so self-conceited that we cannot help others:

> Bear ye one another's burdens, and so fulfil the law of Christ. (Gal. 6:2)

---

5 Let this mind be in you, which was also in Christ Jesus:

Now Paul tells us how we are to carry out these objectives. We are to have the "mind of Christ" (1 Cor. 2:16). Since the scriptures teach that we already have the mind of Christ, we must make practical application. We must renew our minds, and let the mind of Christ tell us what to do:

> For which cause we faint not; but though our outward man perish, yet the inward man is renewed day by day. (2 Cor. 4:16)

> And be renewed in the spirit of your mind. (Eph. 4:23)

> And have put on the new man, which is renewed in knowledge after the image of him that created him. (Col. 3:10)

> And be not conformed to this world: but be ye transformed by the renewing of your mind, that ye may prove what is that good, and acceptable, and perfect, will of God. (Rom. 12:2)

The only way sure way to be obedient to the Lord and follow the scripture is to let the mind of Christ direct your decisions. You still have a "carnal mind" (Rom. 8:7), so you must learn to "yield" to the Spirit instead of the flesh.

---

6 Who, being in the form of God, thought it not robbery to be equal with God:

Here is "the mind of Christ." And what follows is a description of His humility, shown by His submissive mind.

"The form of God" emphasizes Jesus' true humility. If anyone had reason to get glory and honor, it was Jesus! He was, *and is,* God. And

God is the only Being that can truly pat Himself on the back and not sin while doing it. He can brag and say great things of Himself and not be full of pride! Everything He says about Himself is true, and He is deserving of worship.

Man, on the other hand, cannot speak well of himself without sinning because he is *not* deserving of worship. His very nature is evil, and self-promotion is his very downfall. Lucifer had this problem. When he lifted himself up, he fell (Isa. 14:12).

Jesus is **"the form of God,"** the very "image of God" (2 Cor. 4:4; Heb. 1:1-3; Col. 1:13-15). To look at Jesus Christ is to see the *body* of God. Jesus stated it this way to Philip:

> Jesus saith unto him, Have I been so long time with you, and yet hast thou not known me, Philip? he that hath seen me hath seen the Father; and how sayest thou then, Shew us the Father? (John 14:9)

Notice verse six also states that Jesus **"thought it not robbery to be equal with God."** Even though Jesus was not a thief, He is likened unto a "thief" (Matt. 24:43-44; Luke 12:39-40; 1 Thess. 5:2-4; 2 Peter 3:10; Rev. 3:3, 6:15). Don't forget that He was crucified between two *thieves* (Matt. 27:38). But He did not rob deity from God because He was **"equal with God."** The Jews understood His claim perfectly, and to them, it was considered blasphemy.

> Therefore the Jews sought the more to kill him, because he not only had broken the sabbath, but said also that God was his Father, making himself equal with God. (John 5:18)

---

7 But made himself of no reputation, and took upon him the form of a servant, and was made in the likeness of men:

8 And being found in fashion as a man, he humbled himself, and became obedient unto death, even the death of the cross.

"No reputation" means that from His birth to His death, there was not a trace of self-exaltation or pride of reputation in Jesus. He did not try to make a name for Himself, nor did He guard what He said for sake of building a good reputation.

He was also in **"the form of a servant"** in that He was a servant of God. This servitude was prophesied in many Old Testament passages (Isa. 42:1, 49:6, 53:11; Zech. 3:8). The focus of the Lord Jesus was serving and *ministry:*

> Even as the Son of man came not to be ministered unto, but to minister, and to give his life a ransom for many. (Matt. 20:28)

"Made in the likeness of men" means Jesus Christ is the Saviour of men because He *is* a man. Compare this phrase with John 1:14; Rom. 1:3, 8:3; Gal. 4:4, and Heb. 2:14-17. He is 100 percent God and 100 percent man. He is the "mediator between God and men" (1 Tim. 2:5) because He can hold both God's hand and man's hand.

Notice that Christ's obedience in verse eight is connected to His **"death."** This connection is important because it defines the perfection of Christ and magnifies His holiness and refusal to sin. Jesus "was in all points tempted like as we are, yet without sin" (Heb. 4:15). He was not a robot that had no choice but to do right. He was a man with a *will to choose;* that could either do what He wanted or what God wanted:

> Saying, Father, if thou be willing, remove this cup from me: nevertheless not my will, but thine, be done. (Luke 22:42)

Jesus' perfection was not in the fact that He was sinless. His perfection came through His obedience to the Father in carrying out the Father's will:

> For it became him, for whom are all things, and by whom are all things, in bringing many sons unto glory, to make the captain of their salvation perfect through sufferings. (Heb. 2:10)

> Though he were a Son, yet learned he obedience by the things which he suffered; And being made perfect, he became the author of eternal salvation unto all them that obey him. (Heb. 5:8-9)

> And he said unto them, Go ye, and tell that fox, Behold, I cast out devils, and I do cures to day and to morrow, and the third day I shall be perfected. (Luke 13:32)

His humble obedience ("as a lamb" – Isa. 53:7) lead Him to one of the most shameful and humiliating deaths imaginable **– "the death of the cross."** He was stripped completely naked, beaten to near death, had His beard pulled out (Isa. 50:6), and was nailed to the cross to suffer for sins that He hadn't committed. And He went through the entire ordeal without opening His mouth (Isa. 53:7; 1 Peter 2:23).

---

9 Wherefore God also hath highly exalted him, and given him a name which is above every name:
10 That at the name of Jesus every knee should bow, of *things* in heaven, and *things* in earth, and *things* under the earth;
11 And *that* every tongue should confess that Jesus Christ *is* Lord, to the glory of God the Father.

Because Jesus Christ humbled Himself (John 10:18) the Father exalted Him (verses 9-11). He was not merely exalted, but **"highly exalted."** His exaltation is manifested by:

1. His exalted name
2. His exalted place in judgment
3. His exalted recognition

First, the Father has given Him an exalted *name*. The name of Jesus is **"above every name,"** including the name of Mary. In fact, even Jael, the wife of Heber, is said to be blessed "above women" (Judg. 5:24), while Mary is only blessed "among women" (Luke 1:28).

Second, He is exalted in *judgment*. At His name every knee will bow at the judgment. Jesus Himself affirmed His place in judgment:

> For the Father judgeth no man, but hath committed all judgment unto the Son. (John 5:22)

> And hath given him authority to execute judgment also, because he is the Son of man. (John 5:27)

> He that rejecteth me, and receiveth not my words, hath one that judgeth him: the word that I have spoken, the same shall judge him in the last day. (John 12:48)

You see, there will be no excuses at the judgment. Men will not be judged by the hypocrites in the church, or by the pastor that ran off with the secretary. They will be judged by a perfect man – Jesus Christ.

> Because he hath appointed a day, in the which he will judge the world in righteousness by that man whom he hath ordained; whereof he hath given assurance unto all men, in that he hath raised him from the dead. (Acts 17:31)

Like I've heard sung in the following song, everyone will eventually be a believer:

There is no God some folks may say,

Won't go to church or pray,

But when they die what they shall find

Will surely change their mind.

Third, notice that He is exalted in *recognition*. Every man, including God-denying agnostics and atheists, will have to confess **"that Jesus Christ is Lord."** So will all the devils of hell – **"things under the earth."** See Matt. 8:29 for a cross-reference.

The phrase "Jesus is Lord" is a popular slogan for many Charismatic churches in America because they teach that you can lose your salvation. They believe if you confess that "Jesus is Lord" that proves you are saved. This misconception comes from 1 Cor. 12:3 – "no man can say that Jesus is the Lord, but by the Holy Ghost." But they are misreading 1 Cor. 12:3 and misapplying Phil. 2:11. The confession of Phil. 2:11 is **"Jesus Christ is Lord"** while the confession of 1 Cor. 12:3 is "Jesus is THE Lord" (emphasis added). The two are different. There are many lords (1 Cor. 8:5) and many "christs" (Matt. 24:23, 24; Luke 2:26). All unsaved people can confess what every Charismatic claims – that Jesus is Lord, but only true born-again Christians know that "Jesus Christ is THE Lord" (1 Cor. 12:3).

---

12 Wherefore, my beloved, as ye have always obeyed, not as in my presence only, but now much more in my absence, work out your own salvation with fear and trembling.

13 For it is God which worketh in you both to will and to do of *his* good pleasure.

Because Jesus Christ is exalted and has a **"name which is above every name,"** we are to be obedient to Him, for He *is* Lord.

"Work out your own salvation" does not say "work for your own salvation." Verse thirteen makes it clear that this verse is no teaching works are a part of salvation. It does teach, however, that we are to

"work out" some details in our Christian lives. In other words, we need to *work out* what God has already *worked in.*

Every Christian has his own personal walk with the Lord. And that personal walk with God should be the most important thing for him. One way to guard and protect that relationship is by fearing the Lord (verse twelve).

"Fear and trembling." There should still be a holy fear of God in our lives. Even though "perfect love casteth out fear" (1 John 4:18), this fear of God is healthy.

> The fear of the LORD is clean, enduring for ever: the judgments of the LORD are true and righteous altogether. (Ps. 19:9)

> The fear of the LORD is a fountain of life, to depart from the snares of death. (Prov. 14:27)

The Christian can experience the fear of God and the love of God simultaneously. The relationship between father and child demonstrates this seeming paradox. The child loves the father and knows that the father loves him, yet he also fears his father's discipline. The Lord does not want us to be afraid of Him to the extent that we fear to commune with Him, but He does want us to fear Him to the extent that we will be obedient. Our obedience to the Lord is for our benefit and profit, as well as our chastisement (Heb. 12:10).

"To do of his good pleasure" is why you were created – for *His* pleasure, not your own:

> Thou art worthy, O Lord, to receive glory and honour and power: for thou hast created all things, and for thy pleasure they are and were created. (Rev. 4:11)

You will never truly find pleasure in this life until you find it by pleasing God. You must lose your life to find it. You must die to self to truly live. These are undeniable Christian truths.

---

14 Do all things without murmurings and disputings:
15 That ye may be blameless and harmless, the sons of God, without rebuke, in the midst of a crooked and perverse nation, among whom ye shine as lights in the world;
16 Holding forth the word of life; that I may rejoice in the day of Christ, that I have not run in vain, neither laboured in vain.

The Israelites did their share of murmuring and complaining while they wandered in the wilderness (Ex.16:7; Num. 14:27; Ps. 106:25). So did the wicked people of Enoch's day (Jude 15). Perhaps modern American Christians have them both beat in this department. Since the children of Israel are our example (1 Cor. 10:10-11), we better take heed. The Lord does not like this attitude, and it often leads to **"disputings."**

Being **"blameless and harmless"** are not characteristics of those who are murmuring and disputing. You are a bad testimony if you murmur and complain. The unsaved world watches Christians and how they treat one another. If we can't get along with each other, we will be ineffective, and our light will not shine through the darkness.

"The sons of God, without rebuke" implies that you can be a son of God *with* rebuke. In other words, if you don't **"work out your own salvation"** and don't quit murmuring and disputing, you will be a bad testimony for the Lord. Instead of shining **"as lights in the world,"** you will bring reproach (1 Tim. 3:7) upon the "name of Christ" (2 Tim. 2:19).

Verse fifteen teaches that this world is **"crooked and perverse."** Furthermore, the Bible teaches that this world is engrossed in spiritual darkness (John 3:19; Col. 1:13). Your job as a Christian is to **"shine as lights"** by reflecting the light of the "Sun of righteousness" (Mal. 4:2).

The moon is a type of the church because it reflects the light of the sun (Job 25:5 and Song 6:10).

How do we shine? – by **"holding forth the word of life"** (verse sixteen). The scriptures are called **"the word of life"** because they are alive and impart everlasting life (Heb. 4:12; James 1:21). For someone to think that the words of life could be bound by the limitations of *time* is unbiblical. The *inspiration* of the Bible is of no use if it is not *preserved*. You can't hold **"forth the word of life"** if you don't have those words! The teaching of an inspired King James Bible is sound in logic and doctrine.

"That I may rejoice in the day of Christ" means that Paul wanted the Philippians to do well, so he could rejoice when he got to the judgment seat of Christ (note - **"day of Christ"**). From Paul's vantage point, their testimony and obedience to the Lord demonstrated whether or not Paul's work among them was profitable. (See also 1 Thess. 3:5 and Gal. 4:11).

---

17 Yea, and if I be offered upon the sacrifice and service of your faith, I joy, and rejoice with you all.

18 For the same cause also do ye joy, and rejoice with me.

We have already seen how the submitted mind relates to Christ (verses 1-11). What follows (verses 17-30) are the examples of Paul, Timothy, and Epaphroditus.

"If I be offered" is a reference to Paul's dying (see 2 Tim. 4:6). He had no trouble being a living or dying sacrifice for the believers at Philippi (see 1:20). Paul even counted it as **"joy"** because he submitted his life unto God. He allowed the Lord to have control and receive the glory. And if that had meant death, Paul would have had no problem accepting it.

Verse eighteen states the underline Christian experience – **"joy."** But keep in mind the context includes suffering and death!

---

19 But I trust in the Lord Jesus to send Timotheus shortly unto you, that I also may be of good comfort, when I know your state.

20 For I have no man likeminded, who will naturally care for your state.

21 For all seek their own, not the things which are Jesus Christ's.

22 But ye know the proof of him, that, as a son with the father, he hath served with me in the gospel.

23 Him therefore I hope to send presently, so soon as I shall see how it will go with me.

24 But I trust in the Lord that I also myself shall come shortly.

"To send Timotheus shortly" implies that either Timothy may have been visiting Paul in prison (see 1:1), or that Paul was going to send Timothy to the Philippians and then have him report back **("when I know your state")**. Paul spoke well of his young "son" in the faith. He trusted Timothy to act as he himself would have acted on that visit. Timothy became a great pastor and leader because he was first a good follower. His Old Testament counterparts were men like Joshua and Elisha.

Verse twenty-one is a rather harsh but true statement: **"For all seek their own, not the things which are Jesus Christ's."** He said this because Timothy was not this way. But most people are. Most Christians are more concerned with the god of *self*. If Jesus fits into their agenda, He can come along. But if not, they are determined to follow **"their own"** plans for life.

The phrase **"son with the father"** is a proof text for Roman Catholic priests being called "father." But like most of Rome's doctrines, it has no substantiation.

First, there is no record of Timothy or any other Christian in the New Testament calling Paul "father." Second, the religious designation of "father" has always been connected to black-robed priests who worshipped idols (Judg. 17:5-13). Third, no Roman Catholic priest ever "begot" anyone in the faith (1 Cor. 4:15; Philem. 10). They wouldn't know how to lead a soul to Christ if their lives depended on it. And finally, Timothy followed Paul. Roman Catholics and Greek Orthodox churches do not follow Paul. They don't even teach the plan of salvation that Paul preached (Rom. 10:9-13).

"I also myself shall come shortly" is another indication that Paul was imprisoned twice (see also 1:19). If this verse does indicate his release (Acts 28) then he was imprisoned again before his death (2 Tim. 4).

---

25 Yet I supposed it necessary to send to you Epaphroditus, my brother, and companion in labour, and fellowsoldier, but your messenger, and he that ministered to my wants.

Next, we have the example of Epaphroditus – the messenger that came from the Philippian church and brought an offering to Paul (Phil. 4:18).

Notice the words that describe him: **"brother," "companion," "fellowsoldier,"** and **"messenger."** And because he **"ministered,"** he was also a "minister."

Men like Epaphroditus are scarce. Maybe we don't have many Pauls or Timothy's today, because we have few men like Epaphroditus to assist in the ministry.

Let's learn from Epaphroditus's submissive attitude:

1. He was a **"brother."** He was a brother by the new birth into the family of God. That meant he was not a backstabber or an enemy. He was there with Paul because he loved him.

2. He was a **"fellowsoldier."** He knew how to "fight the good fight of faith" (1 Tim. 6:12). He wasn't timid or weak in his Christian life. He fought the world, the flesh, and the devil. He was a good soldier (2 Tim. 2:3-4).

3. He was a **"companion."** In other words, he took sides with Paul instead of against him. He was loyal. Some Christians are only known by what they are against and not what they are for. We need to have balance like Epaphroditus.

4. He was a **"messenger."** He came from Philippi with the offering that they sent (Phil. 4:18). He reported their progress to Paul and delivered their messages to him. We, as Christians, need to be messengers. Like John the Baptist was a "voice," we need to be a voice for God.

5. He was a minister **("ministered to my wants").** He took his job seriously and helped Paul in prison. Being a minister (whether in the spiritual or physical sense) is one of the greatest callings in the world (Matt. 20:26-28).

---

26 For he longed after you all, and was full of heaviness, because that ye had heard that he had been sick.

27 For indeed he was sick nigh unto death: but God had mercy on him; and not on him only, but on me also, lest I should have sorrow upon sorrow.

Verse twenty-six gives us more insight into the character of Epaphroditus. He was not overly concerned about himself. Instead, he was concerned about the Philippians. He had become deathly ill but was more upset about the Philippian's knowledge of his illness than the actual illness itself. He did not want them worrying about him. Apparently Epaphroditus was sick long enough for word to get back to the Philippians; a truth that also indicates his illness was an extended one.

Both Timothy and Paul were often sick (2 Cor. 12:9-10; 1 Tim. 5:3). The faith-healing movement of the Charismatics is not biblical. Paul and Timothy were not healed of their infirmities. Also, the gift of apostolic healing (Mark 16:18) ceased when the nation of Israel rejected the gospel (Acts 28). The *sign gifts* (including tongues, casting out devils, and healing) were to convince the nation of Israel that Jesus really was the risen Messiah. Note:

For the Jews require a sign, and the Greeks seek after wisdom. (1 Cor. 1:22)

Wherefore tongues are for a sign, not to them that believe, but to them that believe not: but prophesying serveth not for them that believe not, but for them which believe. (1 Cor. 14:22)

---

28 I sent him therefore the more carefully, that, when ye see him again, ye may rejoice, and that I may be the less sorrowful.
29 Receive him therefore in the Lord with all gladness; and hold such in reputation:
30 Because for the work of Christ he was nigh unto death, not regarding his life, to supply your lack of service toward me.

Paul sent Epaphroditus **"carefully."** In other words, Paul wanted him to be careful because Epaphroditus was not in good health.

He then mentions the key word **"rejoice"** (verse twenty-eight). He knew they would rejoice when they saw Epaphroditus and received this epistle. At which point, Paul himself would **"be the less sorrowful."** It would comfort him in his affliction when Epaphroditus returned and encouraged the Philippians.

"Hold such in reputation" may indicate that Epaphroditus was an elder of the Philippian church (compare this with Gal. 2:2; 1 Thess. 5:13 and 1 Tim. 5:7).

"For the work of Christ he was nigh unto death." That work was taking care of the apostle Paul and ministering to him in prison. What the Philippians couldn't do being miles away (their **"lack of service")**, Epaphroditus could. He didn't have a lofty position in the world's estimation, but it meant a great deal in the sight of God. We need more Christians who are not concerned with position but rather with priority.

"Not regarding his life" means that Epaphroditus was living the Christian life by dying to self. He found life by not regarding his own.

> For whosoever will save his life shall lose it: and whosoever will lose his life for my sake shall find it. (Matt. 16:25)

Philippians Chapter 3

1 Finally, my brethren, rejoice in the Lord. To write the same things to you, to me indeed *is* not grievous, but for you *it is* safe.

"Finally, my brethren" is not really the conclusion of the letter. He is using the word finally much like many preachers do today (i.e., "Hang on for a little longer, I've got a few more things to say.").

"Finally, my brethren, rejoice in the Lord." The key word of this epistle is emphasized again – **"rejoice"** (see 1:4, 18, 25,26; 2:2, 17, 28).

"For you it is safe." Heeding the commands of the Lord (and **"rejoice in the Lord"** *is* a command) is always prudent. Safety comes when regarding God's statues:

Hold thou me up, and I shall be safe: and I will have respect unto thy statutes continually. (Ps. 119:117)

"Rejoice in the Lord." We are to **"rejoice in the Lord,"** not in men or in our circumstances. People can fail and disappoint us, and circumstances can often be turned against us. This verse is like 1 Thess. 5:18 – "In every thing give thanks . . ." In other words, while you can't always rejoice *because of* everything that happens to you (even "Jesus wept" – John 11:35) you can always rejoice **"in the Lord"** Himself even in the worst of times. Remember, Paul was writing this epistle while in prison.

---

2 Beware of dogs, beware of evil workers, beware of the concision.

"Beware of dogs." Paul is not warning the Philippians about four legged Fidos. The word *dog* in the Bible is used in a defaming and vilifying manner. In some cases, sodomites are called dogs (Deut. 23:18). Other times a dog may refer to a worthless, no-good person (1 Sam. 24:14; 2 Sam. 9:8; 2 Kings 8:13). Jews used the word dog to describe *Gentiles* (Matt. 15:26). Here, Paul is likely warning the sheep of Philippi about false preachers and teachers. Phillips (124) reminds us that "God's people are not dogs, but sheep. Dogs wreak havoc among sheep." Note the cross references:

> His watchmen are blind: they are all ignorant, they are all dumb dogs, they cannot bark; sleeping, lying down, loving to slumber. Yea, they are greedy dogs which can never have enough, and they are shepherds that cannot understand: they all look to their own way, every one for his gain, from his quarter. (Isa. 56:10-11)

> Give not that which is holy unto the dogs, neither cast ye your pearls before swine, lest they trample them under their feet, and turn again and rend you. (Matt 7:6)

> Beware of false prophets, which come to you in sheep's clothing, but inwardly they are ravening wolves. (Matt. 7:15)

> But there were false prophets also among the people, even as there shall be false teachers among you, who privily shall bring in damnable heresies, even denying the Lord that bought them, and bring upon themselves swift destruction. (2 Peter 2:1)

> But it is happened unto them according to the true proverb, The dog is turned to his own vomit again; and the sow that was washed to her wallowing in the mire. (2 Peter 2:22)

"Beware of evil workers." While **"dogs"** refer to false preachers and teachers, **"evil workers"** has a broader meaning. David mentioned **"evildoers"** as those who would not keep God's commands (Ps. 119:115), and Paul wrote about false brethren who professed salvation but did not produce good works (Titus 1:16). Paul's imprisonment was called an "evil work" in 2 Tim. 4:18, and James connected "every evil work" with envying, strife, and confusion (James 3:16). **"Evil workers"** are those who work evil, and you are to **"beware"** (be aware) of them. These wicked people are a dominant part of our society and culture. The ever-increasing iniquity in these days has almost a numbing effect on a Christian's sense of vigilance.

"Beware of the concision." Three warnings are given back-to-back. Here **"the concision"** points to the Jewish fanatics that were proselytizing Gentiles. The word **"concision"** means "to cut off" (Webster's 1828) and is obviously connected with circumcision (see verse three).

---

3 For we are the circumcision, which worship God in the spirit, and rejoice in Christ Jesus, and have no confidence in the flesh.

In other words, Paul was stating that they (he and Timothy – 1:1) were the Jews who really worshiped God, in contrast to **"the concision"** who only had "a form of godliness." Jesus Himself taught that true worship was more than religious ceremonies and observed rituals:

And he said unto them, Full well ye reject the commandment of God, that ye may keep your own tradition. (Mark 7:9)

Making the word of God of none effect through your tradition, which ye have delivered: and many such like things do ye. (Mark 7:13)

God is a Spirit: and they that worship him must worship him in spirit and in truth. (John 4:24)

Worshipping God **"in the spirit"** is possible for the child of God because "he that is joined unto the Lord is one spirit" (1 Cor. 6:17). Paul is stating a simple Christian truth about genuine worship (a truth which has been distorted and twisted even by so-called Christian churches). True worship has little to do with the outward appearance. It concerns the heart, the seat of all devotion. Worship is a spiritual matter *contrary* to **"the flesh"** (verses 3-4). We know this is Paul's emphasis because of the next few verses.

---

4 Though I might also have confidence in the flesh. If any other man thinketh that he hath whereof he might trust in the flesh, I more:
5 Circumcised the eighth day, of the stock of Israel, *of* the tribe of Benjamin, an Hebrew of the Hebrews; as touching the law, a Pharisee;
6 Concerning zeal, persecuting the church; touching the righteousness which is in the law, blameless.

In verse four Paul gives his credentials according to the Jewish mindset of the day. The **"confidence"** he mentions has to do with the pride and self-righteousness that Jews had in their religious upbringing. When he says, **"I more,"** he is bragging that he was a better Pharisee than most.

Paul did everything that the Law and religious tradition of his day said to do. His credentials were as follows:

1. He was circumcised the eighth day (Gen. 17:12).
2. He came from a true blood line (from Benjamin).
3. He took his religion seriously ("**Hebrew of the Hebrews**").

4. He was a Pharisee – "Of the various Jewish sects existing in his day, the Pharisees were the most intensely orthodox." (Ironside, 67). They were very righteous on the outside (Matt. 5:20).

5. He was zealous enough about what he believed to persecute Christians.

6. He was blameless under the Old Testament Law. Note that "blameless" does not mean "sinless." If a person obeyed the Law, he would be considered "blameless" (see Luke 1:6).

---

7 But what things were gain to me, those I counted loss for Christ.

The **"things"** are listed in verses 4-6. At one time, all those religious works were considered **"gain"** to Paul. He believed that the outward deeds of his self-righteous works earned him favor with God. But when the Lord appeared to him (Acts 9), he understood that salvation was "not by works of righteousness which we have done, but according to his mercy" (Titus 3:5).

"I counted loss" shows Paul's true repentance. The word **"counted"** is connected to the word *imputed* which means "to charge; to attribute; to set to the account of" (Webster's 1828). Paul did not count his religious credentials (his works) for anything but **"loss."** He admitted his good works (however admired and acclaimed) would not save him or give him a relationship with Christ. Truthfully, if a person does not give up his self-righteousness and count it as loss he will never be saved.

---

8 Yea doubtless, and I count all things *but* loss for the excellency of the knowledge of Christ Jesus my Lord: for whom I have suffered the loss of all things, and do count them *but* dung, that I may win Christ,

---

"Yea doubtless" affirms the seriousness of Paul's statement. He is certain about what he is saying. Below is a breakdown of verse eight:

1. Paul counted all things loss as far as salvation is concerned.
2. He further counted all things loss as far as knowing Jesus Christ better.
3. Paul was striving for an *excellent* knowledge of Jesus Christ, not just knowledge.
4. Counting things as loss relates to **"suffering the loss of all things."**
5. He viewed **"all things"** on the same level as **"dung."**
6. His goal was not only winning a race (1 Cor. 9:24-27; Heb. 12:1) but also getting closer with Jesus Christ Himself.

---

9 And be found in him, not having mine own righteousness, which is of the law, but that which is through the faith of Christ, the righteousness which is of God by faith:

"Found in him…" Being **"found in him"** is truly the only hope sinners have. When we were born into this world, we were born **"in Adam"** (1 Cor. 15:22), headed for hell in our sinful condition. Neither good works nor self-righteousness could change that fact. Only **"the faith of Christ"** could take us out of Adam and put us into Christ. When we trusted Christ and exercised faith in what Jesus did for us on Calvary, our faith was counted or imputed as righteousness. Note the corresponding verses:

> For ye are all the children of God by faith in Christ Jesus. (Gal. 3:26)

> But to him that worketh not, but believeth on him that justifieth the ungodly, his faith is counted for righteousness. (Rom. 4:5)

A person must have **"the righteousness of God"** to pass the judgment. The only way to get this righteousness is by faith. It cannot be earned, bought, or received *without* faith. While Jesus is the "Saviour of all men" (1 Tim. 4:10), this righteousness of God is only "upon all them that believe" (Rom. 3:22). If a person does not believe in Jesus Christ's atonement for his sins, he will remain in Adam and die and go to hell with his own worthless righteousness. This is why Paul used the term **"dung."**

---

10 That I may know him, and the power of his resurrection, and the fellowship of his sufferings, being made conformable unto his death;

Now Paul takes verse ten a little further than verse nine. Compare this to how he deals with salvation in verse seven and sanctification in verse eight. Here he repeats those truths. Verse nine is salvation while verse ten is sanctification.

"That I may know him." Paul was not saying that he had never known Christ. He claimed to have known the Lord (1 Cor. 2:2; 2 Tim. 1:12; Heb. 10:30). Paul is describing a desire for deeper knowledge as he spoke of in verse eight.

Most Christians are satisfied with their knowledge of the Lord. We are to know *about* Him by what the Bible says about Him, but we should also strive for a personal knowledge of God on an intimate level. Paul desired to ever deepen that part of his relationship. He wanted to know Christ better.

"And the power of his resurrection." This power is available to a Christian through the Holy Ghost. Every Christian has the same power inside of him that "raised up Christ from the dead." Note:

But if the Spirit of him that raised up Jesus from the dead dwell in you, he that raised up Christ from the dead shall also quicken your mortal bodies by his Spirit that dwelleth in you. (Rom. 8:11)

This **"power of his resurrection"** comes with a cost – suffering and death (see the verse). There can't be a resurrection without death, and there can't be death without suffering. Too many Christians want a crown without a cross, a John without a Judas, a revelation without a Patmos, and a resurrection without a death. If you really want to know Jesus Christ, you must follow Him. If you are going to follow Him, you must travel the paths He took:

> And he said to them all, If any man will come after me, let him deny himself, and take up his cross daily, and follow me. For whosoever will save his life shall lose it: but whosoever will lose his life for my sake, the same shall save it. (Luke 9:23-24)

Notice the last word in verse ten – **"death."** The Christian who wants God's power in his life must learn to die. Paul said, **"I die daily"** (1 Cor. 15:31). Death to sin, the deeds of the flesh, and especially *self-* will are required for a Christian to live a resurrected life. Paul exhorted Christians to put these truths into practice (Rom. 6:1-4).

---

11 If by any means I might attain unto the resurrection of the dead.
12 Not as though I had already attained, either were already perfect: but I follow after, if that I may apprehend that for which also I am apprehended of Christ Jesus.

While verse eleven sounds as if Paul is doubting his own resurrection, we know this cannot be the case (1 Cor. 15:51-57; 1 Thess. 4:13-18). The phrase **"resurrection <u>of</u> the dead"** refers to *all* the dead rising. When the scripture speaks of the resurrection of Christ, the phrase used is **"resurrection <u>from</u> the dead"** not **"of"** the dead (see Acts 4:2; Rom. 8:11; 10:7; 1 Cor. 15:12, 20; Gal. 1:11). The wording **"from the dead"** is chosen because Jesus came out *from* the dead *before* the **"resurrection of the dead."** Thus, Christ's resurrection proves that He is not a sinful man, but a man who could by-pass the judgment and come up **"from"** the dead.

The context explains what Paul was doubting:

1. The conditional word **"if"** (verse eleven) relates to Paul's willingness to suffer and die (verse ten).
2. The word **"attain"** is connected with a reward that Paul could get for his suffering. Note the word **"prize"** (verse fourteen) and the cross reference below:

And if children, then heirs; heirs of God, and joint-heirs with Christ; if so be that we suffer with him, that we may be also glorified together. For I reckon that the sufferings of this present time are not worthy to be compared with the glory which shall be revealed in us. (Rom. 8:17-18)

3. While living, Paul had not **"attained"** his reward yet (verse twelve). It will be given at the judgment seat of Christ (which is part of the first resurrection).
4. Rewards at the resurrection are implied throughout the scripture. There is even mention of a "better resurrection" (Heb. 11:35).

"Not as though I had already attained." There are two applications within this verse. First, Paul is saying that he hasn't received the prize yet because the crowns are not given until the day of Jesus' appearing (2 Tim. 4:8). But he is also implying that he isn't satisfied in his walk with the Lord because he says, **"either were already perfect."**

The word **"perfect"** in the Bible does *not* mean *sinlessness*. **"Perfect"** is used to express completion. Webster defines perfect as:

Finished; complete; consummate; not defective; having all that is requisite to its nature and kind; as a perfect statue; a perfect likeness; a perfect work; a perfect system.

Below are the corollary verses that define this perfection.

These are the generations of Noah: Noah was a just man and perfect in his generations, and Noah walked with God. (Gen. 6:9)

Let your heart therefore be perfect with the LORD our God, to walk in his statutes, and to keep his commandments, as at this day. (1 Kings 8:61)

But the high places were not removed: nevertheless Asa's heart was perfect with the LORD all his days. (1 Kings 15:14)

There was a man in the land of Uz, whose name was Job; and that man was perfect and upright, and one that feared God, and eschewed evil. (Job 1:1)

Be ye therefore perfect, even as your Father which is in heaven is perfect. (Matt. 5:48)

Jesus said unto him, If thou wilt be perfect, go and sell that thou hast, and give to the poor, and thou shalt have treasure in heaven: and come and follow me. (Matt. 19:21)

"But I follow after..." (verse twelve). Notice the forward progression of Paul's attitude. He goes on to develop this thought in verse thirteen.

"If that I may apprehend that for which also I am apprehended of Christ Jesus." Paul is saying that he is trying to "get a hold of" or "catch" that which has gotten a hold of him. Or, that he is trying to fulfill his calling in Christ to reach the point that the Lord wants him to reach.

---

13 Brethren, I count not myself to have apprehended: but *this* one thing *I do*, forgetting those things which are behind, and reaching forth unto those things which are before,

---

"I count not myself to have apprehended." Paul admits that he hasn't perfected his Christian walk. He isn't proud or high-minded and knows he hasn't reached the peak of his relationship with the Lord. His humility is apparent, and his goal is seen in the rest of the verse.

"But this one thing I do." Notice the singularity of the statement. Phillips (page 143) commenting on D. L. Moody:

> D. L. Moody, almost as busy a man as Paul in the work of Christ, used to say, "It is better to say, 'This one thing I do,'" than to say, 'These forty things I dabble with.'"

Christians often mistake being busy for being spiritual. Doing many things for the Lord may be admirable, but they might cause you to lose sight of the **"one thing"** that you are to be doing. It is possible to serve the Lord while being out of fellowship with Him. How soon do we forget the story of Mary and Martha? Martha was busy serving while Mary was sitting at the feet of Jesus:

> Now it came to pass, as they went, that he entered into a certain village: and a certain woman named Martha received him into her house. And she had a sister called Mary, which also sat at Jesus' feet, and heard his word. But Martha was cumbered about much serving, and came to him, and said, Lord, dost thou not care that my sister hath left me to serve alone? bid her therefore that she help me. And Jesus answered and said unto her, Martha, Martha, thou art careful and troubled about many things: But one thing is needful: and Mary hath chosen that good part, which shall not be taken away from her. (Luke 10:38-42)

"Forgetting those things which are behind." This counsel is great for anyone, but especially for those with scarred pasts. There are three things that we are to do with the past:

1. Look at it.
2. Learn from it.
3. Leave it.

If you don't learn to leave the past, it will constantly haunt you. Because of Paul's wicked past, he learned to leave it by looking to the future – "Looking unto Jesus the author and finisher of our faith" (Heb. 12:2).

"And reaching forth unto those things which are before." You can't reach forward until you've let go of that which is behind you. This is repentance in action – turning from the past and to the future.

---

14 I press toward the mark for the prize of the high calling of God in Christ Jesus.

Paul undoubtedly watched some of the Olympic Games in his day since he lived where the games would have been played. He often used illustrations that related to those games or their rewards (1 Cor. 9:24-26; Heb. 12:1, 2). The Christian is typified as a(n)

1.   Farmer (1 Cor. 3:7-8).
2.   Soldier (2 Tim. 2:3-4).
3.   Priest (1 Peter 2:5).
4.   Athlete (1 Cor. 9:24-26; Gal. 2:2; 5:7; Heb. 12:1).

Verse fourteen should be the incentive for the Christian life. There is always more *to do for* Christ and more *to learn about* Christ. And there is a prize to win. All too often Christians simply quit in their Christian walk because they think they have already attained (see verse twelve). These contented Christians become wise in their own conceit (Prov. 26:12) "and their ears are dull of hearing" (Matt. 13:15). They may be saved, but their walk with Jesus Christ is dull and boring. Many times, they live in the past and reflect on what the Lord *used* to do and how the Lord *used* to work. They have become ineffective and lukewarm (Rev. 3:16) and wouldn't feel the hand of God if it touched them on the shoulder. Judgment is the only remedy (1 Peter 4:17).

---

15 Let us therefore, as many as be perfect, be thus minded: and if in any thing ye be otherwise minded, God shall reveal even this unto you.
16 Nevertheless, whereto we have already attained, let us walk by the same rule, let us mind the same thing.

In verse fifteen Paul uses the word **"perfect"** to describe himself even after he said that he wasn't perfect (verse twelve). This usage confirms that perfection is a state the Christian should strive to obtain – to those who are following Christ to that end.

"Be thus minded." In other words, those who are perfect will apply verses 10-14. And if anyone thinks any other way **("be otherwise minded"),** God will show him that he should have the same goal and attitude that Paul just explained **("God shall reveal even this unto you.")**.

The last part of verse fifteen is a good reminder for Christians who may be a little further down the road of faith than others. Instead of condemning or preaching to the stragglers, they should have patience with them. The others will catch up after a while. And if they don't, that is between them and the Lord. You can't change their minds for them.

"Nevertheless, whereto we have already attained." In other words, "Don't lose any ground." Look where the Lord has brought you and don't go back! Scripture warns us about giving **"place to the devil."** (Ephesians 4:27).

"Same rule, let us mind the same thing." True biblical Christian unity is a wonderful thing. It is so great that the devil tries to mimic it for his own exploits. Unfortunately, because Christians know that they should be in accord, many fall prey to ecumenism or nondenominationalism. But true Christian unity is always Bible based and never carnal.

> Endeavouring to keep the unity of the Spirit in the bond of peace. (Eph. 4:3)

> Till we all come in the unity of the faith, and of the knowledge of the Son of God, unto a perfect man, unto the measure of the stature of the fulness of Christ. (Eph. 4:13)

---

17 Brethren, be followers together of me, and mark them which walk so as ye have us for an ensample.
18 (For many walk, of whom I have told you often, and now tell you even weeping, *that they are* the enemies of the cross of Christ:
19 Whose end is destruction, whose God *is their* belly, and *whose* glory *is* in their shame, who mind earthly things.)

In verse seventeen Paul exhorts the Philippians to follow him. There was even a group of Christians from AD 600-970 who were called Paulicians because of their emphasis on Paul's writings (Schaff, 573-576). Notice Paul's exhortation to follow him:

> Wherefore I beseech you, be ye followers of me. (1 Cor. 4:16)

> Be ye followers of me, even as I also am of Christ. (1 Cor. 11:1)

Paul gave these instructions under the inspiration of the Holy Spirit, and they are not to be taken lightly. In fact, Paul was the "apostle of the Gentiles" (Rom. 11:13), and he wrote 14 of the 27 books of the New Testament! We are to gather our core doctrinal beliefs from *his* epistles. Any doctrinal truth that contradicts Pauline revelation (like salvation by works and faith - Matt. 19:16-17; Rev. 22:14; James 2:24; Heb. 6:4-6) is not to be applied in this current age. We are to follow Paul and the revelation that God gave to him. This revelation (among other things) includes the mystery of the body of Christ (Eph. 3:3-6; Col. 1:26-27) and the rapture of the church before the tribulation (1 Cor. 15:51-57; 1 Thess. 4:13-18).

"Mark them" (verse seventeen) is to be taken both negatively and positively.

First, we should mark (or notice) those who are following the Lord and learn from them. One of the greatest lessons a Christian mom or dad can give is to teach by simply living a godly life. Your children will watch how you walk and know whether or not you are walking with the Lord. They can tell if your priorities are Bible based or if they are selfish.

Second, we should mark those who are not following the Lord; those who are **"enemies of the cross of Christ"** (verse eighteen). We are commanded to point out the enemies of the Lord.

> Now I beseech you, brethren, mark them which cause divisions and offences contrary to the doctrine which ye have learned; and avoid them. (Rom. 16:17)

> And if any man obey not our word by this epistle, note that man, and have no company with him, that he may be ashamed. (2 Thess. 3:14)

The text does not imply that we should spend all our energy and effort confronting and correcting everyone. Some ministries are known for what they stand *against* rather than what they stand *for.* We are not to waste God's time pointing out every heretic. If we spent all our time preaching against cults and heresies, we could never fulfill the commission of preaching the gospel of Jesus Christ. However, we must still warn people about falsehoods by teaching people the truth from the Bible. Then they will be apt and able to **"mark them"** on their own.

Notice the characteristics of false teachers in verse nineteen:

1. Their "end is destruction" (see 2 Peter 2:1).
2. Their "God is their belly" (see Isa. 56:11; Ezek. 34:3; Rom. 16:18; 1 Tim. 6:5; Titus 1:11).

3. Their "glory is in their shame" (see James 4:16; Jude 13).
4. They "mind earthly things" (Ps. 17:14; Matt. 16:23; Rom. 8:5-7).

---

20 For our conversation is in heaven; from whence also we look for the Saviour, the Lord Jesus Christ:

21 Who shall change our vile body, that it may be fashioned like unto his glorious body, according to the working whereby he is able even to subdue all things unto himself.

"Our conversation" is never used exclusively for speech or language. Instead, it carries a broader meaning. Webster's 1828 gives one meaning as "the general course of manners; behavior; deportment; especially as it respects morals."

Scripture is abundantly clear that more than speech is implied in the word conversation (see comments under Phil. 1:27).

If **"our conversation is in heaven,"** we should be more heavenly minded than earthly minded. Someone has said, "You can be so heavenly minded that you are no earthly good." But one preacher retorted back, "If you are not heavenly minded, you will not be any good on earth." Amen.

The Bible teaches us that we are to lay up "treasures in heaven" (Matt. 6:20) and that we are to "seek those things which are above" (Col. 3:1). We are to think about heaven and what is in heaven – namely the Lord Jesus Christ.

"We look for the Saviour" *not:*

1. The temple to be rebuilt in Jerusalem.
2. The ten toed confederated kingdom of Daniel.
3. The Antichrist.
4. Sacrificial worship in Israel.
5. The great tribulation.

6. The mark of the beast.
7. A pouring out of the Holy Spirit.
8. The Kingdom of Heaven.

It seems Christians are looking for everything except the Lord's coming! The Bible teaches the imminent return of Christ – that Jesus Christ could come back at any moment. There are no more prophecies that need to be fulfilled before Jesus Christ returns.

The return of Jesus Christ can be divided into two *stages:*

1. The rapture.
2. The revelation.

The word *rapture* comes from the Latin word "raptus" and means "to catch up" or "transport." The Bible word for rapture is "translated" (Heb. 11:5). At the rapture, Jesus Christ will meet the church in the clouds and then take it to heaven. At this time all Christians since the death of Jesus Christ (dead or alive) will be "caught up" (1 Thess. 4:17) to forever be with the Lord.

The *revelation* happens when Jesus Christ physically returns to earth to set up His kingdom. This will be a time of judgment and punishment for non-believers (2 Thess. 1:7-9).

Since Paul is addressing the Christians at Philippi, we know he is speaking of the rapture.

"Who shall change our vile body." When the Lord raptures us, He will complete our salvation. When you were saved, your spirit was born again and your soul was saved, but your body was not. Your body is still corrupt and sinful and will eventually die because of the disease of sin (Rom. 6:23). When the Lord comes again, He will transform our corruptible mortal bodies into a body like unto His. This act will complete our salvation and finalize our adoption:

And not only they, but ourselves also, which have the firstfruits of the Spirit, even we ourselves groan within ourselves, waiting for the adoption, to wit, the redemption of our body. (Rom. 8:23)

"That it may be fashioned like unto his glorious body." Our corruptible bodies of sin will be changed like the glorified body of Jesus Christ. This is done:

1. To make us sinless like Christ.
2. To manifest eternal life in a *physical* sense. These bodies will never die (Rev. 21:4).
3. To make it possible for us to behold God in His holiness and purity (Rev. 22:4).

Since our bodies will be fashioned like the glorified body of Christ, (called a **"spiritual body"** – 1 Cor. 15:44), they will be:

1. Sinless.
2. Flesh and bones (Luke 24:39). Blood is not mentioned in the glorified body of Christ. We know sinful "flesh and blood cannot inherit the kingdom of God" (1 Cor. 15:50).
3. Able to eat food (Luke 24:42-43; Rev. 19:9).
4. Able to appear and disappear at will (Luke 24:31).
5. Able to travel faster than the speed of light (John 20:17 with Matt. 28:9).
6. Able to pass through solid objects (John 20:26; Joel 2:8).

What an amazing truth to grasp! One day we will be like Jesus Christ! No more sin, no more pain, no more death, no more shortcomings! And greatest of all – we shall behold Him!

Beloved, now are we the sons of God, and it doth not yet appear what we shall be: but we know that, when he shall appear, we shall be like him; for we shall see him as he is. (1 John 3:2)

PHILIPPIANS CHAPTER 4

---

1 Therefore, my brethren dearly beloved and longed for, my joy and crown, so stand fast in the Lord, *my* dearly beloved.

Wiersbe's outline for chapter four is God's peace—4:1-9, God's power—4:10-13, and God's provision—4:14-23.

"Therefore, my brethren" is Paul's second closing of this letter to the Philippians (see 3:1 for the first and 4:8 for the last).

"Dearly beloved." Paul uses this phrase eight times in his epistles (twice in this verse), articulating his love and concern for these saints.

"And longed for." Paul had a longing to see them again in person – something he mentioned several times in this epistle (see Phil. 1:25 and 2:24).

"My joy and crown" has both practical and doctrinal applications. First, the Philippians were Paul's joy because he rejoiced to hear how they progressed in their Christian walk. Knowing that the Lord had used him to reach these people was a blessing to Paul, as was the fact that the Lord was using him to help them to continue to grow in their faith.

The doctrinal meaning reaches out to the judgment seat of Christ. Notice that these converts of the apostle Paul are called his **"crown."** This implies that one of the crowns at the judgment seat of Christ will be representative of souls we have led to Jesus Christ. Note the cross reference:

> For what is our hope, or joy, or crown of rejoicing? Are not even ye in the
> presence of our Lord Jesus Christ at his coming? (1 Thess. 2:19)

Below are the five crowns that are mentioned by name in scripture:

1. The crown of righteousness – for those who "love his appearing" (2 Tim. 4:8).
2. The crown of rejoicing – for those who win others to Christ (Phil. 4:1; 1 Thess. 2:19).
3. The crown of life – for those who endure temptation or give their life for Christ (James 1:12; Rev. 2:10).
4. The incorruptible crown – for those who are faithful running their race (1 Cor. 9:24-25).
5. The crown of glory – for pastors who are faithful to their calling (1 Peter 5:1-4).

"Stand fast in the Lord." This phrase expresses a fixed position as in the word *fastener*. Paul used this phrase often as an encouragement in the Christian battle (1 Cor. 16:13; Gal. 5:1; Phil. 1:27). In other words, once you have learned the basics, just do what you know to do – **"stand fast."** This command seems so simple, yet it is one of the most important. When things get tough, **"stand fast."** When things are confusing, **"stand fast."** When life throws you a curve, **"stand fast."** When trouble and heartache hit, **"stand fast."** Don't lose faith, don't quit, don't give up. Stay in the battle, get up off the ground, and **"stand fast."** In Ephesians we learn about the armor we are to **"stand fast"** with:

> Stand therefore, having your loins girt about with truth, and having on the
> breastplate of righteousness; And your feet shod with the preparation of the
> gospel of peace; Above all, taking the shield of faith, wherewith ye shall be able

to quench all the fiery darts of the wicked. And take the helmet of salvation, and the sword of the Spirit, which is the word of God. (Eph. 6:14-17)

If you stand on your own strength, you will fall every time. You are to stand fast **"in the Lord."** David knew this truth when he faced Goliath. He said, "I come to thee in the name of the LORD of hosts" (1 Sam. 17:45).

---

2 I beseech Euodias, and beseech Syntyche, that they be of the same mind in the Lord.

Evidently these two ladies (assuming these are women's names) had some difficulty getting along. Paul is not overly harsh with them, but he does address the problem. I imagine they were embarrassed when this letter was read to the entire church. Hopefully, they made things right.

Being **"of the same mind"** does not mean everyone is going to get along. With all the different personalities and backgrounds, it is not uncommon for people to cross one another every now and again. However, the scripture teaches us to love one another as Christian brothers and sisters and to try to get along:

> Be of the same mind one toward another. Mind not high things, but condescend to men of low estate. Be not wise in your own conceits. (Rom. 12:16)

> If it be possible, as much as lieth in you, live peaceably with all men. (Rom. 12:18)

> And to esteem them very highly in love for their work's sake. And be at peace among yourselves. (1 Thess. 5:13)

> Finally, be ye all of one mind, having compassion one of another, love as brethren, be pitiful, be courteous: (1 Peter 3:8)

---

3 And I intreat thee also, true yokefellow, help those women which laboured with me in the gospel, with Clement also, and *with* other my fellowlabourers, whose names are in the book of life.

A yoke is a piece of wood fastened over the necks of two oxen to allow them to pull together. A **"yokefellow"** is a person that is in a yoke with you. Paul identified these Philippians as yoked together with him for the work of God.

"Those women which laboured with me in the gospel." While the Bible insistently forbids women from holding an office in the church (pastor or deacon), it never forbids women from working in the church. In fact, there were faithful women in both Jesus' ministry and Paul's (Luke 23:27, 49, 55; Rom. 16:12-16).

"With Clement also." Roman Catholic tradition says that this Clement was a pope at Rome. But that folklore is purely speculation. Clement is simply classified with the women workers and **"fellowlabourers."**

"Whose names are in the book of life." This reference is the only mention of the **"book of life"** outside of Revelation (where it is mentioned seven times). Though Jesus does not mention the book by name, He does declare that the disciples "names are written in heaven" (Luke 10:20). The Lord Jesus could have been referring to their names being on the twelve foundations of New Jerusalem (Rev. 21:14) or that their names were in the book of life. This statement by Paul is very important because it confirms the eternal security of the church age Christian. The Bible assures all whose names are in the book of life are protected from burning in the lake of fire:

And whosoever was not found written in the book of life was cast into the lake of fire. (Rev. 20:15)

---

4 Rejoice in the Lord alway: *and* again I say, Rejoice.

Once again Paul restates his theme for the entire letter – rejoice in the Lord!

The phrase **"in the Lord"** specifies *Who* our rejoicing should be centered around. If we are simply to *rejoice* in anything, the source of a Christian's happiness would be the same as those in the world. We are to joy and rejoice *in Jesus Christ!* Our joy is not in ourselves or each other, or our blessings from God. Our joy is to be in Christ Jesus Himself. When the believer rejoices in Christ he draws strength, as Nehemiah says, **"the joy of the Lord is your strength"** (Neh. 8:10).

Note verse four retains the older English **"alway"** instead of "always" like all the modern versions. The King James' use of "alway" is another instance where our Bible's wording demonstrates more depth. Here **"alway"** can mean "at all times" (like always) and "in every kind of way."

---

5 Let your moderation be known unto all men. The Lord *is* at hand.

This is the only occurrence of the word **"moderation"** in the Bible. Another form "moderately" is found in Joel 2:23. It means "having restraint and not being excessive." Christians are to demonstrate their **"moderation"** and not participate the excess of sin that is prevalent in the world around us (see 1 Peter 4:3-4).

"The Lord is at hand" could refer to the imminent return of Christ, but in this instance, I think it indicates His omnipresence. He is **"at hand"** in the sense that "The Lord is standing by" (Ironside, page 90).

Wiersbe (page 94) outlines the next verses as right praying (verses 6-7), right thinking (verse eight), and right living (verse nine).

---

6 Be careful for nothing; but in every thing by prayer and supplication with thanksgiving let your requests be made known unto God.

7 And the peace of God, which passeth all understanding, shall keep your hearts and minds through Christ Jesus.

"Be careful." Here again the wording of the King James text is far superior to the other "Bibles." The new versions erroneously replace **"careful"** with "anxious," but the right word is **"careful"** because Christians *should* be "anxious" (e.g., eager) about certain things such as,

1. The Lord's return.
2. Having a closer walk with the Lord.
3. Seeing people get saved.

By keeping the correct word, we understand that **"careful"** (i.e., *full of care)* is an admonition against worry. "John Wesley is reported to have said that he did not know which dishonored God the most – to worry, which is really to doubt His love and care, or to curse and swear." (Ironside, page 97). The Christian is to pray rather than worry. The Lord illustrated this truth in a special way with His disciples:

> Therefore I say unto you, Take no thought for your life, what ye shall eat, or what ye shall drink; nor yet for your body, what ye shall put on. Is not the life more than meat, and the body than raiment? Behold the fowls of the air: for they sow not, neither do they reap, nor gather into barns; yet your heavenly Father feedeth them. Are ye not much better than they? (Matt. 6:25-26)

Instead of being consumed with worry, we should pray about everything – the small problems as well as the big ones. Worry is the natural consequence for a prayerless Christian. We are commanded to pray, rather than worry. Until you pray about the matter, worry will remain.

"Prayer and supplication" are listed separately because supplication is a separate component of prayer. Prayer can describe all aspects of communicating with God: worship, adoration, thanksgiving, supplication, requests, and any other communion. In **"supplication"** a Christian asks God to *supply* a specific need (see Acts 1:14 and Eph. 6:18).

"With thanksgiving." Many people forget that prayer should include thanking the Lord for everything He has done for us. A grateful heart will not go unnoticed with the Lord (Luke 17:17-19).

"And the peace of God." Many also incorrectly interpret this verse to mean that we will get our prayers answered just as we desire. This interpretation illustrates one of the two problems people generally have with prayer:

1. They don't understand how to pray according to the Bible or what to expect as a result.
2. They don't pray at all.

To rectify the first problem, a Christian must consider *all* verses on prayer and not just "whatsoever ye shall ask in my name, that will I do" (John 14:13). Verse seven does not promise that you will get what you are praying for. But it does teach all prayers are answered – just not necessarily in the way you would like them to be answered.

The assurance of verse seven is that the **"peace of God"** will keep you from going crazy! You do not have to let worry and anxiety control your life. You can pray and leave the problem in God's hands.

"The peace of God" is incomprehensible. We are unable to understand how it really works. We just know that it does. One of the greatest proofs for biblical Christianity is the fact that millions of

Christians testify to God's grace in answered prayer and peace! As Phillips (page 163) states:

> Nothing can ruffle the peace of God. It is a calm beyond all storms, a rest beyond all strife, a haven beyond all tempestuous seas. The peace of God is majestic and sublime.

Of course, this **"peace of God"** comes **only "through Christ Jesus."** No one else can give this peace. Religious leaders can't give it. Priests and religious teachers can't supply it. Families can't will it for future generations. Only Jesus Christ can bring the peace of God.

> Therefore being justified by faith, we have peace with God through our Lord Jesus Christ. (Rom. 5:1)

> And, having made peace through the blood of his cross, by him to reconcile all things unto himself; by him, I say, whether they be things in earth, or things in heaven. (Col. 1:20)

---

8 Finally, brethren, whatsoever things are true, whatsoever things are honest, whatsoever things *are* just, whatsoever things *are* pure, whatsoever things *are* lovely, whatsoever things *are* of good report; if *there be* any virtue, and if *there be* any praise, think on these things.

Now Paul is going to conclude by enumerating those things we are to think about – all of them righteous, uplifting, and positive.

First, he lists the "thoughts that promote inner character" (Phillips, page 165).

Truth is mentioned first to contrast falsehood's lies. We are to think about things that are **"true"** rather than those that are *false*. There is no profit in corrupting our minds by studying every heresy and cock-eyed idea. We are to study the word of God in *truth*.

But truth without virtue or loveliness can lead to realism that is tarnished and filthy, so the list continues.

"Whatsoever things are honest." Honesty is antithetical to lying and will eventually reveal the truth.

"Whatsoever things are just" are not *evil* or *shady* or *crooked* in any way.

Now Paul moves on to "thoughts that promote inner cleanliness" (Phillips, page 167).

"Whatsoever things are pure" contrasts those things that are unclean. The Bible takes great effort to point out the differences between the clean and the unclean, the pure and the impure:

> Unto the pure all things are pure: but unto them that are defiled and unbelieving is nothing pure; but even their mind and conscience is defiled. (Titus 1:15)

> Lay hands suddenly on no man, neither be partaker of other men's sins: keep thyself pure. (1 Tim. 5:22)

"Whatsoever things are lovely" would include things that are beautiful and gracious - like God's creation. We should fill our minds with that which is lovely instead of that which is degrading and filthy.

"Whatsoever things are of good report." Bad news or gossip always spreads faster than good news. Most *true-life* stories that we are captivated by are *not* of good report. Just because a story is true does not make it fit to think about! People are brutally murdered every day, but does that mean we should spend hours on end filling our minds with that *news?* True or not, we are not to justify thinking on things of *bad* report for the sake of knowledge.

The verse concludes with two qualifying standards with which to judge the things you might allow into your mind.

"If there be any virtue." Virtue has to do with moral goodness (Webster). Ruth was called a "virtuous woman" (Ruth 3:11), and as Christians we are to "add to your faith virtue" (2 Peter 1:5).

"If there be any praise." What we think about should be praiseworthy, thus eliminating perverse and vain thoughts. Thoughts not worthy of praise, virtue, and attention should be abandoned at once.

"Think on these things." The mind has always been the battlefield. What you put in your mind has a tremendous effect on how you live. Your mind is affected by what you see, what you hear, and what you read. As Christians it is our responsibility to guard our minds and get rid of thoughts or imaginations that are contrary to God and His word.

> For though we walk in the flesh, we do not war after the flesh: (For the weapons of our warfare are not carnal, but mighty through God to the pulling down of strong holds;) Casting down imaginations, and every high thing that exalteth itself against the knowledge of God, and bringing into captivity every thought to the obedience of Christ. (2 Cor. 10:3-5)

---

9 Those things, which ye have both learned, and received, and heard, and seen in me, do: and the God of peace shall be with you.

In verse nine the apostle Paul exhorts us to live right and says we are to follow him (see 3:17). I believe it was Bob Jones Sr. who said, "It is never a compromise to go as far as you can on the right road with anyone." Paul certainly went down the right road.

"Seen in me." We concur with Ravenhill (page 71) that "there is a world of difference between knowing the word of God and knowing the God of the Word." And though knowledge may be a means, it is never the end. In fact, by itself "knowledge puffeth up" (1 Cor. 8:1). Paul believed his personal testimony was important enough that the Philippians should learn from it. He was so confident with his testimony that he often told Christians to "follow" him (2 Thess. 3:7-9; 1 Cor. 11:1).

Paul is saying in verse nine that our fellowship **("the God of peace shall be with you")** is based on living right and obeying God.

Unfortunately, many Christians today want fellowship with both God and the world. They want to be both sanctified *and* sensual; holy *and* unholy. James sums up this aberrant theology by stating:

> Out of the same mouth proceedeth blessing and cursing. My brethren, these things ought not so to be. Doth a fountain send forth at the same place sweet water and bitter? (James 3:10-11)

---

10 But I rejoiced in the Lord greatly, that now at the last your care of me hath flourished again; wherein ye were also careful, but ye lacked opportunity.

Paul rejoiced in the Lord because of the generosity of the Philippians. He expounded on the teaching of spiritual giving in 2 Cor. 9:10-15. Note the following:

1. Paul had a genuine burden and need.
2. Paul prayed about his need.
3. The Philippians sent an offering by Epaphroditus (verse eighteen).
4. The offering caused Paul to glorify and praise God.
5. So, the Philippians caused God to receive glory and praise while Paul was blessed, and the work of the ministry continued – the sum of which is an "unspeakable gift" from God (2 Cor. 9:15).

---

11 Not that I speak in respect of want: for I have learned, in whatsoever state I am, *therewith* to be content.
12 I know both how to be abased, and I know how to abound: every where and in all things I am instructed both to be full and to be hungry, both to abound and to suffer need.

"In respect of want" means that Paul is not writing because he is trying to solicit something from the Philippians.

"Whatsoever state" includes being "abased" or "abounded" (verse twelve). Dr. Ruckman (page 455) said, "Success is getting what you want; happiness is wanting what you get." Paul's attitude of contentment was not realized overnight. He made this statement after going through the trials listed in 2 Corinthians 11 (prison, death, beating, shipwreck, being robbed, exhaustion, hunger, nakedness, burdens of the ministry). Would you be content with only food and clothes?

> But godliness with contentment is great gain. For we brought nothing into this world, and it is certain we can carry nothing out. And having food and raiment let us be therewith content. (1 Tim. 6:6-8)

"How to be abased...and...how to abound" can both be equally troublesome. I've heard a wealthy Christian say, "One of the greatest temptations is prosperity." The Lord probably doesn't give most of us great sums of money because we simply couldn't handle it. If most Christians had a lot of money, the money would possess them, instead of them possessing it!

But being **"abased"** and "humbled" is much less appealing. Most want the crown without the cross; the resurrection without the death; the upper room without Gethsemane.

How would you react if God took everything away from you? Could you handle it? How would you react if God prospered you well beyond what you could ever imagine? Could you handle it? In the Old Testament, Joseph is a good example of someone who was both abased and then later made to abound. He was broken before he received the blessing (Matt. 14:19)!

---

13 I can do all things through Christ which strengtheneth me.

Verse thirteen is one of the greatest Bible promises for a Christian. Nothing a child of God does for the Lord is accomplished through his own self-confidence or natural ability. Rather, all things are done **"through Christ"** because He is the *One* who gives the Christian strength. The promise of the verse is,

1.   Personal, for each of His children.
2.   All-encompassing because being all powerful, God can dispense His strength and power to those children that are in His will.

Jesus said unto him, If thou canst believe, all things are possible to him that believeth. (Mark 9:23)

3.   Valid only **"through Christ."** Our strength alone is not good enough. We need *His* strength to become our strength.
4.   **"Through Christ"** not "through Him" as found in the modern versions. The absence of "Christ" is a *bad* reading. The King James text is supported with Greek manuscript evidence (all three families – Hesychian, Byzantine, and Western, plus Athanasius, Chrysostom, and Cyprian cite it – Dr. Ruckman, page 456).

When you are faced with a trial or temptation, get the victory by claiming this promise **"through Christ."** You can overcome sin and be victorious through Jesus Christ.

And they overcame him by the blood of the Lamb, and by the word of their testimony; and they loved not their lives unto the death. (Rev. 12:11)

---

14 Notwithstanding ye have well done, that ye did communicate with my affliction.

15 Now ye Philippians know also, that in the beginning of the gospel, when I departed from Macedonia, no church communicated with me as concerning giving and receiving, but ye only.

16 For even in Thessalonica ye sent once and again unto my necessity.

17 Not because I desire a gift: but I desire fruit that may abound to your account.

In verse fourteen the word **"communicate"** means giving specifically to God's work (see also Gal. 6:6; 1 Tim. 6:18, and Heb. 13:16). Paul commends them for helping him. At a time when other churches were slack in giving, the Philippians were faithful on many occasions (verse sixteen). Their giving not only supplied his need but also allowed the Lord to bless them. Through giving they laid up "treasures in heaven" (Matt. 6:19-20).

The gospel ministry is to be supported by the saints. Believers are to supply the money for those who do the Lord's work. The Bible compares this plan to that of sheep and a shepherd. The sheep are to support the shepherd. While the shepherd cares and looks out for the sheep, he also lives off what they provide for him. Paul taught this truth in the following other scriptures:

> Even so hath the Lord ordained that they which preach the gospel should live of the gospel. (1 Cor. 9:14)

> Let him that is taught in the word communicate unto him that teacheth in all good things. (Gal. 6:6)

> Let the elders that rule well be counted worthy of double honour, especially they who labour in the word and doctrine. For the scripture saith, Thou shalt not muzzle the ox that treadeth out the corn. And, The labourer is worthy of his reward. (1 Tim. 5:17-18)

This system of giving and receiving teaches dependence on God. The saints must have faith enough to do their duty, and the minister must have faith enough to trust God to supply the need. The shepherd is to be faithful in teaching the sheep this truth (albeit with the right motive – verse seventeen), and the sheep must be faithful in obeying the Lord. When either side fails to obey, the Lord is dishonored by the lack of trust in Him.

---

18 But I have all, and abound: I am full, having received of Epaphroditus the things *which were sent* from you, an odour of a sweet smell, a sacrifice acceptable, wellpleasing to God.

Though Paul learned to live in a contented state (verse eleven), he was also genuinely thankful for what the Philippians sent through Epaphroditus.

Notice he compared their offering to an Old Testament sacrifice which sent out a sweet smell. Giving is a spiritual sacrifice that we can offer up to the Lord. It pleases the Lord when we give with the right motive and attitude.

Every man according as he purposeth in his heart, so let him give; not grudgingly, or of necessity: for God loveth a cheerful giver. (2 Cor. 9:7)

---

19 But my God shall supply all your need according to his riches in glory by Christ Jesus.

This verse is another great Bible verse for Christians to memorize. Paul was thankful for the Philippians' obedience to God in supplying his need, and he declared that the Lord will do the same for them.

Notice that the verse does not say, "God shall supply all your *greed*." While driving down the interstate on a trip, my wife and I passed a huge RV motor home. I jokingly commented to my wife, "Now that's what we need." She quickly retorted, "If we needed it, the Lord would have given us one because the Bible says He will provide all our needs." Yes, I was rebuked!

God will provide for you *as He sees fit* because He knows what you require more than you do. Christians are like babies who cry with equal aggressiveness when they need to be changed or when they simply want to be held. Some of our so-called needs are not needs at all! If you require it, God will provide it! Keep in mind that this promise is given to an obedient church that is taking care of a minister. Compare this to Gal. 6:6-10.

How can God supply your need? He can do it because He is God. His riches are endless.

---

20 Now unto God and our Father *be* glory for ever and ever. Amen.
21 Salute every saint in Christ Jesus. The brethren which are with me greet you.
22 All the saints salute you, chiefly they that are of Caesar's household.
23 The grace of our Lord Jesus Christ *be* with you all. Amen.

"God and our Father" is a phrase that is used throughout Paul's epistles (see Gal. 1:4; 1 Thess. 1:3; 3:11). The phrase is not implying that God is separate from the Father but rather emphasizing that God *is* our Father. Notice how it is worded in another verse:

> To the end he may stablish your hearts unblameable in holiness before <u>God, even our Father</u>, at the coming of our Lord Jesus Christ with all his saints. (1 Thess. 3:13) *[emphasis added]*

This type of phrasing is also used when speaking of the Lord Jesus Christ:

> Looking for that blessed hope, and the glorious appearing of the great God and our Saviour Jesus Christ. (Titus 2:13)

Titus 2:13 is not teaching that Jesus is separate from God, but rather that **"the great God"** *is* **"our Saviour Jesus Christ."**

"The brethren which are with me greet you." Paul's brethren were both bound with him in prison and free in the palace (Phil. 1:13). Verse twenty-two mentions those **"of Caesar's household."**

This small epistle concludes in verse twenty-three as though it was written not merely from Paul's hand but from the Lord's. And since the Bible is divinely inspired, it indeed was. While the Bible had human penmen, it was authored by God Himself. Paul is speaking on behalf of the *One* who "moved" him (2 Peter 1:21) to write this inspired letter.

If you have a Bible with a postscript, it will say this letter was written "to the Philippians from Rome by Epaphroditus." Now while postscripts are not inspired scripture, they can be helpful. Even though the postscript states that Epaphroditus wrote the letter, there is no doubt that Paul is the author. Most of Paul's epistles were written by others (except Galatians and Philemon – Gal. 6:11; Philem. 19). Inspiration often refers to "verbal inspiration" – where the human author dictates the inspired word, and another person transcribes it (see Jer. 36:18). Thank God that He promised to preserve His inspired words after they were verbally spoken!

> The words of the LORD are pure words: as silver tried in a furnace of earth, purified seven times. Thou shalt keep them, O LORD, thou shalt preserve them from this generation for ever. (Ps. 12:6-7)

COLOSSIANS
INTRODUCTION

The book of Colossian has 4 chapters, 95 verses, and 1979 words (Vance, 218).

Colossians was written by the apostle Paul when he was in prison in Rome. In fact, Ephesians, Philippians, Colossians, and Philemon were all written and delivered at about the same time: approximately AD 64.

The city of Colosse was in western Asia Minor on the banks of the Lycus River. It was eleven miles from Laodicea and close to Hierapolis (see Col. 4:13). While there were many Jews in the region, this church seems to have been mostly Gentiles (note "the uncircumcision of your flesh" – Col. 2:13).

The apostle Paul did not start the church at Colosse nor is there any record that he ever went there. Perhaps it spawned out of Paul's ministry at Ephesus, which had a tremendous effect on the surrounding towns. In Ephesus Paul taught and preached the word of God daily in the school of Tyrannus. The impact of those meetings no doubt, would have also reached Laodicea, Hierapolis, and Colosse:

> But when divers were hardened, and believed not, but spake evil of that way before the multitude, he departed from them, and separated the disciples, disputing daily in the school of one Tyrannus. And this continued by the space of two years; so that all they which dwelt in Asia heard the word of the Lord Jesus, both Jews and Greeks. (Acts 19:9-10)

Col. 1:7 and 4:12 seem to indicate that Epaphras was the pastor of this church. While in prison with Paul, Epaphras related the condition of the saints at Colosse. Paul then composed this letter, addressing these issues, and sent it to them by the hand of Tychicus and Onesimus (Col. 4:7-9).

We agree with Wiersbe (page 104) that the "main theme" of the book of Colossians is "the preeminence of Jesus Christ" (Col. 1:18; 3:11). But because the Colossian church was plagued with "intellectualism, ritualism, legalism, mysticism, and asceticism" (Phillips, page 7), there is also a *second theme* of rebuke and warning concerning heresies and false teachings. Paul used the word of God to expose these unorthodox practices. As Dr. Ruckman observed (page 464) Paul refuted the heresies of:

1. Ebionite teachings (those who followed Christ's teachings but rejected His deity).

2. Essene teachings (those who through "will worship" denied the flesh and trusted their good works for salvation.)

3. Judiazers (those who tried to corrupt Christianity with left over Judaism).

4. Philosophers (who attempted to leaven the word of God by philosophical carnality).

Paul mentions Laodicea *five* times in this book, implying perhaps a prophetic significance to this letter. Laodicea is a type or picture of the end of the church age. And just as the rapture follows the Laodicean age, the book following Colossians (1 Thessalonians) is a book where the rapture is mentioned in all five chapters! So, this is a book that is much needed in the Laodicean church period, and we would do well to read it with the same fervor as did the first century Christians of Colosse.

Wiersbe (page 101) outlines the book as: Chapter 1: Doctrine: Christ's Preeminence Declared, Chapter 2: Danger: Christ's Pre-eminence Defended, Chapters 3-4: Duty: Christ's Preeminence Demonstrated.

COLOSSIANS CHAPTER 1

---

1 Paul, an apostle of Jesus Christ by the will of God, and Timotheus *our* brother,

2 To the saints and faithful brethren in Christ which are at Colosse: Grace *be* unto you, and peace, from God our Father and the Lord Jesus Christ.

Though Paul is the primary author of the epistle to Colosse, Timothy is also given credit for it **("and Timotheus")**. So, the letter is actually from both of them.

"By the will of God" confirms Paul's apostleship and his actions thereafter. Several times he attests that his calling was of God:

> But I certify you, brethren, that the gospel which was preached of me is not after man. For I neither received it of man, neither was I taught it, but by the revelation of Jesus Christ. (Gal. 1:11-12)

> Paul, an apostle, (not of men, neither by man, but by Jesus Christ, and God the Father, who raised him from the dead. (Gal. 1:1)

> Paul, a servant of Jesus Christ, called to be an apostle, separated unto the gospel of God. (Rom. 1:1)

> Who gave himself a ransom for all, to be testified in due time. Whereunto I am ordained a preacher, and an apostle, (I speak the truth in Christ, and lie not;) a teacher of the Gentiles in faith and verity. (1 Tim. 2:6-7)

Whereunto I am appointed a preacher, and an apostle, and a teacher of the Gentiles. (2 Tim. 1:11)

For I speak to you Gentiles, inasmuch as I am the apostle of the Gentiles, I magnify mine office. (Rom. 11:13)

Paul's epistles are written with authority under the inspiration of God Almighty. Similarly, when a God-called preacher delivers a message, he should preach it as he received it from the Lord. Though preached by a fallible human, the Lord sanctions and honors messages from His word. And any mistakes fall squarely on the preacher's shoulders.

"To the saints and faithful brethren" address both the believers in general and those who are faithfully serving the Lord.

Unfortunately, even a saint can live like a sinner. In fact, all saints are still sinners by nature, although they are saints through the new birth. In the Old Testament, *sinner* and *saint* have more rigid definitions than what you find in the book of Romans (see1 Sam. 15:18; Prov. 11:31; 13:6 with Rom. 3:23; 5:12).

"Grace...and peace, from God our Father and the Lord Jesus Christ." This phrase suggests that the letter is not merely from Paul and Timothy, but also from the Lord Himself!

---

3 We give thanks to God and the Father of our Lord Jesus Christ, praying always for you,

4 Since we heard of your faith in Christ Jesus, and of the love *which ye have* to all the saints,

---

In verse three Paul expressed thanks to God for the church at Colosse, lifting them up in prayer. We are commanded to pray for our brethren in Christ:

Brethren, pray for us. (1 Thess. 5:25)

Now I beseech you, brethren, for the Lord Jesus Christ's sake, and for the love of the Spirit, that ye strive together with me in your prayers to God for me. (Rom. 15:30)

Praying always with all prayer and supplication in the Spirit, and watching thereunto with all perseverance and supplication for all saints. (Eph. 6:18)

The knowledge that someone is praying for you brings great comfort and assurance.

"Since we heard of your faith." The church of the Colossians was established as a result of the great revival at Ephesus (Acts 19:9-10). And since Paul and Timothy were never in Colosse, this verse indicates they may have heard of their faith from Epaphras (see verse eight and 4:12). Paul says he and Timothy heard of their faith in Christ, and their love toward the brethren.

Those two attributes are marks of real, authentic Christianity. Jesus *never* said people would know his disciples by how they dressed or what heresies they stood against. Rather, He identified *love* as the number one trait:

By this shall all men know that ye are my disciples, if ye have love one to another. (John 13:35)

---

5 For the hope which is laid up for you in heaven, whereof ye heard before in the word of the truth of the gospel;

6 Which is come unto you, as *it is* in all the world; and bringeth forth fruit, as *it doth* also in you, since the day ye heard *of it*, and knew the grace of God in truth:

In verse five we learn that our faith and love is founded in **"hope."** That *hope* is the reason for right behavior.

Unlike the way the word is used today, the word hope in the Bible does not signify something that *might* happen. Rather, hope is the assurance of something that will *definitely* happen in the future – in this verse, our **"hope"** is an inheritance **"in heaven"** (see 1 Peter 1:4).

"The word of the truth of the gospel" is a noteworthy phrase because these three words – word, truth, and gospel – are found together. Without *words* you couldn't hear **"truth."** And without the **"gospel,"** the words of truth would have no personal effect on you. It is the gospel of Jesus Christ that brings the words of salvation to the soul.

"As it is in all the world" points to the great influence and outreach of the Ephesus revival (see Acts 19).

"Bringeth forth fruit" has an order:

1. The gospel of truth is preached.
2. The Colossians heard it **("the day ye heard of it")**.
3. They experienced the **"grace of God."**
4. That word now is bringing **"forth fruit."**

The word of God goes out - the seed is sown, and later it brings forth fruit in those that receive it:

> But he that received seed into the good ground is he that heareth the word, and understandeth it; which also beareth fruit, and bringeth forth, some an hundredfold, some sixty, some thirty. (Matt. 13:23)

> For this cause also thank we God without ceasing, because, when ye received the word of God which ye heard of us, ye received it not as the word of men,

but as it is in truth, the word of God, which effectually worketh also in you that believe. (1 Thess. 2:13)

---

7 As ye also learned of Epaphras our dear fellowservant, who is for you a faithful minister of Christ;

8 Who also declared unto us your love in the Spirit.

In verse seven Paul mentions Epaphras for the first time. He is said to be,

1. Dear unto Paul.

2. A **"fellowservant."**

3. A **"faithful minister."**

4. A messenger who **"declared unto us your love in the Spirit."**

So, it appears that Epaphras may have been the pastor of the church at Colosse, and also the one who told Paul some things about the church. Because of what Epaphras told him, Paul began to pray for them as he did the other churches. Notice his prayer:

---

9 For this cause we also, since the day we heard *it*, do not cease to pray for you, and to desire that ye might be filled with the knowledge of his will in all wisdom and spiritual understanding;

10 That ye might walk worthy of the Lord unto all pleasing, being fruitful in every good work, and increasing in the knowledge of God;

11 Strengthened with all might, according to his glorious power, unto all patience and longsuffering with joyfulness;

"Do not cease to pray" indicates that Paul made prayer a priority – not something he put off or forgot altogether (see also 1 Thess. 2:13,

5:17; 2 Tim. 1:3). Paul did not forget them; he prayed for them often. Phillips outlined this petition as "vision, vitality, and victory" (pages 35-41).

Paul's prayer for the Colossians is quite similar to his prayer for the Ephesians (Eph. 1:16-19).

Paul prayed that they might **"be filled with the knowledge of his will."**

Since the Colossian church was plagued with philosophy and Gnosticism, Paul prayed that they would get the right **"knowledge"** (see also Col. 1:27, 2:3, 3:10, etc.). Nothing is more valuable than knowing the will of God. For someone who is unsaved, the will of God is for him to be saved (2 Peter 3:9). For a Christian, outside of the clear commands in scripture, the will of God can vary individually. We are to make our "calling and election sure" (2 Peter 1:10).

In order to discern the will of God, we need two things.

The first is **"wisdom"** (verse nine). Wisdom is not just an accumulation of facts, but rather the proper use of those facts. The Bible extols wisdom and encourages its acquisition:

Get wisdom, get understanding: forget it not; neither decline from the words of my mouth. (Prov. 4:5)

For wisdom is better than rubies; and all the things that may be desired are not to be compared to it. (Prov. 8:11)

The fear of the LORD is the beginning of wisdom: and the knowledge of the holy is understanding. (Prov. 9:10)

How much better is it to get wisdom than gold! and to get understanding rather to be chosen than silver! (Prov. 16:16)

But of him are ye in Christ Jesus, who of God is made unto us wisdom, and righteousness, and sanctification, and redemption. (1 Cor. 1:30)

The second is **"spiritual understanding"** (verse nine). Spiritual understanding includes discernment. Saved people can be deceived about spiritual things (1 Cor. 6:9; 15:33; Gal. 6:7). To have spiritual discernment, a Christian must know the Bible and be "be filled with the spirit" (Eph. 5:18). Practical application of scripture paired with proper doctrinal understanding leads to good discernment.

Paul's prayer continues, asking that they **"walk worthy of the Lord."**

Paul prays that the Colossians would exemplify the name "Christian." Although no believer is worthy of salvation, we are still called to **"walk worthy"** of it (see Eph. 4:1; 1 Thess. 2:12; 2 Thess. 1:5). And although we are not saved by good works, we are still to do good works after we are saved.

The worth of the believer's walk is not determined by beliefs and creeds, but how well we please the Lord with our lives. Our thoughts, our actions, and our motives should all be to the glory of God. We were created and then saved so we could bring glory and pleasure to the Lord:

Thou art worthy, O Lord, to receive glory and honour and power: for thou hast created all things, and for thy pleasure they are and were created. (Rev. 4:11)

Not only are we to please the Lord with our lives, but we are also to be **"fruitful in every good work."** Bearing fruit is a natural result of a Christian growing in his faith (Gal. 5:22-23).

"Increasing in the knowledge of God." How much better do you know the Lord this year than say, two years ago? What have you learned *from* the Lord, and *about* the Lord lately? The older we get, the more we forget. But spiritually, the more mature we grow in the Lord, the more we should know *about* the Lord, and the more we should *know* the Lord:

> But grow in grace, and in the knowledge of our Lord and Saviour Jesus Christ. To him be glory both now and for ever. Amen. (2 Peter 3:18)

"Strengthened with all might." Of all people, Paul knew how demanding the Christian life could be. He prayed for the Colossians to be strong, so they could "fight the good fight." Of course, the Christian's strength comes from the Lord's **"glorious power"** and not from within himself:

> Finally, my brethren, be strong in the Lord, and in the power of his might. (Eph 6:10)

Paul learned this fact firsthand because of his own infirmities. This strength from God is manifested by **"patience and longsuffering with joyfulness"** (verse eleven). Note the following:

> And he said unto me, My grace is sufficient for thee: for my strength is made perfect in weakness. Most gladly therefore will I rather glory in my infirmities, that the power of Christ may rest upon me. (2 Cor. 12:9)

> But in all things approving ourselves as the ministers of God, in much patience, in afflictions, in necessities, in distresses. (2 Cor. 6:4)

It was the Lord Jesus Himself who experienced this strength to the fullest, maintaining joy even through death, to thus become the conqueror:

> Looking unto Jesus the author and finisher of our faith; who for the joy that was set before him endured the cross, despising the shame, and is set down at the right hand of the throne of God. (Heb. 12:2)

These things have I spoken unto you, that my joy might remain in you, and that your joy might be full. (John 15:11)

---

12 Giving thanks unto the Father, which hath made us meet to be partakers of the inheritance of the saints in light:

13 Who hath delivered us from the power of darkness, and hath translated *us* into the kingdom of his dear Son:

"Giving thanks" to the Lord was something Paul was always careful to do, and we would do well to learn from his example. Prayer should be more than vain repetitions for things we need or want. Prayer should also include praise and thanksgiving to God (Phil. 4:6; Col. 2:7; 4:2; 1 Tim. 4:4).

What was Paul giving thanks to God for? First, he gave thanks for the new birth **("made us meet").**

Therefore if any man be in Christ, he is a new creature: old things are passed away; behold, all things are become new. (2 Cor. 5:17)

Heaven or any **"inheritance of the saints"** is only for those who have been born again, and God alone gives believers the "power to become the sons of God" (John 1:12). Once a man was asked what part he played in his salvation, and he responded, "The running part. I ran, and God came after me."

"The inheritance" entails more than just a home in heaven. It also includes rewards for Christian service given at the judgment seat of Christ (1 Cor. 3:11-15).

"Saints in light." Notice that light relates to saints while darkness is connected with sinners:

And this is the condemnation, that light is come into the world, and men loved darkness rather than light, because their deeds were evil. For every one that doeth evil hateth the light, neither cometh to the light, lest his deeds should be reproved. But he that doeth truth cometh to the light, that his deeds may be made manifest, that they are wrought in God. (John 3:19-21)

He will keep the feet of his saints, and the wicked shall be silent in darkness; for by strength shall no man prevail. (1 Sam. 2:9)

"Who hath delivered from the power of darkness." The Christian has been freed from the evil power that binds an unsaved person. This Satanic darkness (Luke 22:53; 2 Cor. 4:4) blinds the hearts of unbelievers to the truth of the gospel:

Having the understanding darkened, being alienated from the life of God through the ignorance that is in them, because of the blindness of their heart. (Eph. 4:18)

As Christians we must realize that the unsaved world is shrouded in darkness. The lost cannot see the light of Jesus Christ and are blind to the truth. It is no wonder that they do the wicked things they do. What more could you expect from someone bound and controlled by Satan?

"Translated us." To *translate* means to be changed from one state to another. When you were saved, God removed you from the kingdom of darkness and placed you in the kingdom of Jesus Christ.

To open their eyes, and to turn them from darkness to light, and from the power of Satan unto God, that they may receive forgiveness of sins, and inheritance among them which are sanctified by faith that is in me. (Acts 26:18)

This **"kingdom of his dear Son"** is a spiritual kingdom that is entered by the new birth (John 3:1-5) and is *not* the same as the kingdom of heaven. The kingdom of heaven is a *physical* kingdom on earth connected to the Jewish throne of David (Matt. 19:28; Isa. 9:7). The kingdom in Colossians chapter one is the *spiritual* "kingdom of God" (Rom. 14:17).

"Hath translated us" is *past* tense. Our translation has already happened. Christians today are presently in this spiritual kingdom, not waiting to enter it. We are in it now! This kingdom is *not* physical so does not depend on politics, votes, or armed combat for its survival.

In all three instances where the word *translate* is used (or a similar form), the *translation* is better than the *original* (2 Sam. 3:10; Col. 1:13; Heb. 11:5). Isn't it strange that so-called Bible scholars and critics of the King James Only movement missed those cross references? Enoch was certainly better after his translation than before. And who would argue against David's kingdom being was better than Saul's? Surely there could be no dispute that a person is better after he has been translated from Satan's kingdom to God's kingdom! The KJO position is indeed a *biblical* viewpoint regarding the history of Bible inspiration and subsequent preservation.

---

14 In whom we have redemption through his blood, *even* the forgiveness of sins:

It is through God that we have been delivered from Satan's kingdom, and it is **"through his blood"** that we have been redeemed.

Verse fourteen has been corrupted in the new versions like the New International Version (NIV), and the New American Standard Bible (NASB). They omit **"through his blood"** even though the rest of the New Testament teaches redemption is by the blood of Christ (Acts 20:28; Rom. 3:24-25; Eph. 1:7; Heb. 9:12; 1 Peter 1:19-20; Rev. 1:5). Incidentally, the new versions retain **"through his blood"** in Ephesians 1:7. Also, by removing **"through his blood"** it fosters the idea that redemption and the forgiveness of sins are synonymous. They are not! As Dr. Ruckman (474) points out:

Israel was forgiven (Luke 23:34) but not redeemed (Acts 3:19). A man can be forgiven (Matt. 18:32) and go to hell. OT saints were forgiven (Ex. 34:1-8), but none of them were redeemed at that time, or within 400 years of that time (Gal. 4:5).

Forgiveness isn't enough without redemption. Redemption must have the basis to buy and clear the soul. The following verses illustrate this truth:

> But in those sacrifices, there is a remembrance again made of sins every year. For it is not possible that the blood of bulls and of goats should take away sins. (Heb. 10:3-4)

> And every priest standeth daily ministering and offering oftentimes the same sacrifices, which can never take away sins: But this man, after he had offered one sacrifice for sins for ever, sat down on the right hand of God. (Heb. 10:11-12)

God could *forgive* sins because of the blood of animals, but He couldn't *clear* sins or redeem anyone before the death, burial, and resurrection of Christ:

> Keeping mercy for thousands, forgiving iniquity and transgression and sin, and that will by no means clear the guilty; visiting the iniquity of the fathers upon the children, and upon the children's children, unto the third and to the fourth generation. (Ex. 34:7)

It took the pure and precious blood of Jesus Christ to "take away" or redeem us from our sins:

> Forasmuch as ye know that ye were not redeemed with corruptible things, as silver and gold, from your vain conversation received by tradition from your fathers; But with the precious blood of Christ, as of a lamb without blemish and without spot. (1 Peter 1:18-19)

15 Who is the image of the invisible God, the firstborn of every creature:

Paul continues **"giving thanks unto the Father"** (verse twelve) by lifting up and magnifying His redemptive plan. Phillips (46) outlines the rest of the chapter as the deity of Christ (15-17), the death of Christ (20-22), and the demands of Christ (23-29).

"Who is the image of the invisible God" confirms the deity of Jesus Christ in that He is the visible manifestation of God Himself (1 Tim. 3:16). Notice two other verses that use this phrase:

> Who being the brightness of his glory, and the express image of his person, and upholding all things by the word of his power, when he had by himself purged our sins, sat down on the right hand of the Majesty on high. (Heb. 1:3)

> In whom the god of this world hath blinded the minds of them which believe not, lest the light of the glorious gospel of Christ, who is the image of God, should shine unto them. (2 Cor. 4:4)

In other words, if you *saw* God, you would be looking at the Lord Jesus Christ. During His earthly ministry, the Lord Jesus told Phillip that very truth:

> Philip saith unto him, Lord, shew us the Father, and it sufficeth us. Jesus saith unto him, Have I been so long time with you, and yet hast thou not known me, Philip? he that hath seen me hath seen the Father; and how sayest thou then, Shew us the Father? (John 14:8-9)

With the previous verses in mind, it is easy to understand why the Lord is so adamant against idols and images supposedly depicting His likeness (see Ex. 20:4; Lev. 26:1; Deut. 4:16). He *has* an image – the Lord Jesus Christ. And, by the way, Jesus is not a black man, or white man with long flowing blond hair and blue eyes! On His mother's side, He is a Jew of **"the son of David, the son of Abraham"** (Matt 1:1).

Although man was originally created "in the image of God" (Gen. 1:27; 9:6), he never was the *very* image of God. Furthermore, after Adam's sin, we are now born into this world "after *his* image," not God's (Gen. 5:3). The Bible explains the difference between Adam's image and God's image:

> For as in Adam all die, even so in Christ shall all be made alive. (1 Cor. 15:22)

When Adam sinned, the Bible says he died (see Gen. 2:17), even though his body lived to be 930 years old. What died then? Adam's spirit died – the part that could fellowship with God, for "God is a spirit" (John 4:24). Consequently, everyone is born with Adam's image, having a dead spirit and a sinful nature (Eph. 2:1-3), unable to commune with God, or "please God" (Rom. 8:8).

A "natural man" has *no* spiritual connection to God (1 Cor. 2:14). His first birth is no good. He "must be born again" (John 3:7) to restore the fallen image Adam lost.

"The invisible God" cannot be seen with human eyes:

> Who only hath immortality, dwelling in the light which no man can approach unto; whom no man hath seen, nor can see: to whom be honour and power everlasting. Amen. (1 Tim. 6:16)

When the Bible says men saw God (Ex. 24:11; Gen. 16:13; 32:30; Judg. 13:22), what they saw was an *appearance* of God. They could not have seen God's essence, or they would be burned up:

> No man hath seen God at any time; the only begotten Son, which is in the bosom of the Father, he hath declared him. (John 1:18)

For our God is a consuming fire. (Heb 12:29)

God is invisible because you can't see a Spirit (John 4:24). Neither can you see the *human* soul or spirit, only the body. Similarly, God's body – the Lord Jesus – is visible while His soul – the Father, and the Spirit – the Holy Spirit are not.

"The firstborn of every creature" may seem to be a confusing phrase. First, let's see what the verse is *not* saying. **"Firstborn of every creature"** doesn't mean that Jesus was the first being ever created like Jehovah's Witnesses teach. The very next verse clarifies that Jesus Christ is the *Creator*. He could not have created Himself! The meaning is obviously a reference to His authority as the firstborn of God (see verse eighteen – **"firstborn from the dead"**).

Next, notice that the word firstborn is understandable enough. Jesus Christ is Mary's "firstborn son" (Matt. 1:25), connecting the context to the incarnation, when Jesus was begotten. And though there are other "sons of God" (Gen. 6; John 1:12), Jesus Christ was the "only begotten Son" of the Father conceived by the Holy Ghost in a physical sense. So, since Jesus is the firstborn, we can now be born into God's family as new "creatures." Note:

> Therefore if any man be in Christ, he is a new creature: old things are passed away; behold, all things are become new. (2 Cor. 5:17)

> For whom he did foreknow, he also did predestinate to be conformed to the image of his Son, that he might be the firstborn among many brethren. (Rom. 8:29)

Look back at Rom. 8:29 and note that one day all sons of God (Christians) will be "conformed to the image" of Jesus Christ. This *changing* (1 Cor. 15:51) will complete our salvation, and our adoption will be finalized. Then we will know that we are children of God, not merely by faith, but by sight! Our bodies will be changed to be like the Son of God (see Phil. 3:20, 21; 1 John 3:1, 2 and Rom. 8:23).

---

16 For by him were all things created, that are in heaven, and that are in earth, visible and invisible, whether *they be* thrones, or dominions, or principalities, or powers: all things were created by him, and for him:

17 And he is before all things, and by him all things consist.

"For by him were all things created" settles the controversy as to the deity of Jesus Christ. We know that Jesus Christ is God because He is the Creator – **"the everlasting God."**

> Hast thou not known? hast thou not heard, that the everlasting God, the LORD, the Creator of the ends of the earth, fainteth not, neither is weary? there is no searching of his understanding. (Isa. 40:28)

Jehovah God is the Creator, the Holy Spirit is the Creator, and Jesus Christ is the Creator; but they are considered the **"Holy One"** (not two, or three – Isaiah 31:1; Acts 3:14; 1 John 2:20).

To promote their false doctrine, the Jehovah's Witnesses' perverted *Bible,* the New World Translation (NWT), changes verse sixteen to read:

> Because by means of him all [other] things were created . . . All [other] things have been created through him and for him.

Verse sixteen says **"all things"** twice. Not only is Jesus the Creator of everything on the earth, but also of things in heaven, in both the physical and spiritual realms.

"Principalities, or powers" refers to more than mortal rulers (see Eph. 6:12). This verse along with Job 26:13 shows that Satan was created by God. It is an eerie thought to consider that Job 26:13 has been changed in every new version, thus removing the reference to God creating the devil.

"And for him." Everything was made for God and *His* glory. Fulfillment in life comes from bringing glory and honor to the One who made you for Himself:

> Thou art worthy, O Lord, to receive glory and honour and power: for thou hast created all things, and for thy pleasure they are and were created. (Rev. 4:11)

"And he is before all things" is summarized perfectly by John 1:1. He is before all things because He is eternal while time and matter are not. He is also **"before all things"** because of His position. He is to be *exalted* **"before all things."**

"By him all things consist." Scientists think they have found what holds the atom together. They call it the *gluon*. But what keeps the gluon *glued* together? And what keeps the laws of thermodynamics in order? Why should we believe that gravity will continue to work as it has for centuries? Who keeps the earth the exact distance from the sun, so we are not incinerated or frozen? Who gives us the air we breathe? His name is Jesus and he "uphold[s] all things by the word of his power" (Heb. 1:3). It is the Lord Jesus Christ that keeps this universe together, not some mathematical formula. And when the Lord decides to use this earth for kindling wood, it will go up in flames faster than a charcoal grill at a tailgate party (2 Peter 3:10-14).

---

18 And he is the head of the body, the church: who is the beginning, the firstborn from the dead; that in all *things* he might have the preeminence.

In verse eighteen Paul identifies **"the body"** of Christ as **"the church,"** thus showing that there are two definitions for the word *church* in the New Testament. One usage of the word *church* is for a local assembly (Acts 11:22). The other usage is collective for all believers in Jesus Christ (see also Eph. 1:22-23).

"Head of the body" leaves no room for any other potentate, pope, or pastor. Jesus is the head, even if local churches do not acknowledge Him as such:

> And hath put all things under his feet, and gave him to be the head over all things to the church. (Eph. 1:22)

The teaching of the New Testament is that Jesus is the head – the leader and final authority for the church. Pastors of local churches are to be under the authority of the Lord Jesus Christ, and their "rule" is to be in spiritual matters *only* (1 Tim. 5:17). They are to preach the Bible as the final authority, not their opinions, dogmas, pet peeves, or political convictions.

God's ultimate purpose was that Jesus Christ **"might have the preeminence"** in both the spiritual body of Christ and the local assembly (verse eighteen). As Phillips (page 68) aptly states, "Some people give Him *place*...Other people go further and give Him *prominence*...Then a few people give Him *preeminence.*" Unfortunately, many churches today steal the glory from God to exalt man. Many church members think services are to be entertaining and should make people feel good about themselves.

"Firstborn from the dead." While there were others who were resurrected *before* Jesus Christ, there were none who were God's "firstborn" (see Ps. 89:27), and none who rose from the dead by their own power:

> Therefore doth my Father love me, because I lay down my life, that I might take it again. No man taketh it from me, but I lay it down of myself. I have

power to lay it down, and I have power to take it again. This commandment
have I received of my Father. (John 10:17-18)

---

19 For it pleased *the Father* that in him should all fulness dwell;

In other words, "the fulness of the Godhead" (all three persons of
the Triune God) is manifested in Jesus Christ. When Jesus Christ came
to earth, it was a *full* and *complete* display of God:

For in him dwelleth all the fulness of the Godhead bodily. (Col. 2:9)

---

20 And, having made peace through the blood of his cross, by him to reconcile all
things unto himself; by him, *I say*, whether *they be* things in earth, or things in heaven.

21 And you, that were sometime alienated and enemies in *your* mind by wicked works,
yet now hath he reconciled

22 In the body of his flesh through death, to present you holy and unblameable and
unreproveable in his sight:

"Peace through the blood of his cross" speaks of reconciliation.
How an instrument of torture and brutality could bring peace remains
part of the mystery of the cross. What the cross did, however, was to
bridge the gap between sinful man and a holy God. Reconciliation was
made because the sins and iniquities of man were finally punished by an
appropriate sacrifice being made in the sinner's behalf. God's wrath was
vindicated, and man's liberty promised.

But this transaction didn't happen just because of Christ's death.
Notice the verse says, **"through the blood."** At the Passover night in
Egypt, God said, "when I see the blood, I will pass over you…" (Ex.
12:13). The blood brings **"peace"** because it assures us that the
punishment of our sins is complete.

"Things in earth, or things in heaven" probably refers to the redeeming of those alive and those who died prior to the crucifixion of Christ (see Eph. 4:8-9).

"And you." The Bible though the apostle Paul addresses each individual Christian personally. You should never forget where you were when God saved you – lost and deserving of nothing but hell. Don't ever forget the fact that you were the enemy of God and part of the devil's family before you were saved. The things you thought in **"your mind,"** as well as the **"wicked works"** that were manifested outwardly set you *against* God.

"Yet now." Thank God for the "yets" and "buts" of the Bible! To be **"reconciled"** means to be restored to fellowship with God. It is predicated upon belief in the blood atonement of Jesus on the cross. No sinner can be reconciled apart from coming to the cross.

How did Jesus Christ accomplish salvation and reconcile us? Verse twenty-two says, **"in the body of his flesh through death."** You see, Jesus took upon Himself the form of a man (Phil. 2:5-8), so He could die for sinful flesh. When He hung on the cross, all the sins of the world were placed upon Him and He became the embodiment of sin (2 Cor. 5:21). He bore our transgressions upon His own body (Isa. 53:5; 1 Peter 2:24) and died because of the sins we commit. When His sinless blood flowed it testified that the price for sin had been paid. Jesus lived the perfect life we couldn't live. He never sinned and is the only One deserving of heaven (not hell). Anyone who trusts Him can get His righteous life attributed to his own record. For this reason, verse twenty-two says that He can present us **"holy and unblameable and unreproveable in his sight."**

The great hymn-writer Charles Wesley penned it well:

My God is reconciled His pardoning voice I hear
He owns me for His child, I can no longer fear
With confidence I now draw nigh
And Father, Abba Father cry.

---

23 If ye continue in the faith grounded and settled, and *be* not moved away from the hope of the gospel, which ye have heard, *and* which was preached to every creature which is under heaven; whereof I Paul am made a minister.

Now there is a conditional prerequisite in verse twenty-three that has to do, not with the reconciliation (verse twenty-one), but rather with the presenting of the child of God **"unblameable and unreproveable."** Undoubtedly, this takes place at the judgment seat of Christ (2 Cor. 5:10), where believers will literally be presented **"in his sight."** Note the following cross-references:

> That thou keep this commandment without spot, unrebukeable, until the appearing of our Lord Jesus Christ. (1 Tim. 6:14)

> That he might present it to himself a glorious church, not having spot, or wrinkle, or any such thing; but that it should be holy and without blemish. (Eph. 5:27)

> Wherefore, beloved, seeing that ye look for such things, be diligent that ye may be found of him in peace, without spot, and blameless. (2 Peter 3:14)

"Be not moved away" implies that the believer can get away from **"the hope of the gospel"** that we have as Christians. This **"hope"** is connected to "hope" of the rapture (Rom. 8:24, 25; Titus 2:13). Paul is *not* teaching that a Christian can lose his salvation. A Christian can, however, move away in fellowship from the Lord and the very hope that we have as believers. A Christian may move away from the Lord in his fellowship, but he can never move away in his "sonship." No Christian can be "un" born again.

"Preached to every creature which is under heaven" is not saying that Mark 16:15 is fulfilled. Dr. Ruckman (506) rightly states that "Paul is not speaking of the individual proclamation of one individual to another as in Mark 16:15, but is talking about God's proclamation to the human race."

The gospel **"was preached to every creature"** in the sense that it was given to the entire world. The message of the cross is not to a select few, but to *every* person *everywhere*.

---

24 Who now rejoice in my sufferings for you, and fill up that which is behind of the afflictions of Christ in my flesh for his body's sake, which is the church:

25 Whereof I am made a minister, according to the dispensation of God which is given to me for you, to fulfil the word of God;

"Rejoice in my sufferings for you." Paul suffered much for the work of the ministry (2 Cor. 11:23-33). Not only was he afflicted with natural sicknesses and diseases, but Paul also had to combat physical persecution as well.

Nevertheless, he was not consumed with complaining or bitterness. Rather, his attitude was joyful – happy that he could suffer for Christ, and on behalf of other Christians. This attitude was exemplified with the early church (see Acts 5:41-42).

"Fill up that which is behind of the afflictions of Christ." Paul is not saying that he is sacrificially suffering for anyone. Suffering was part of Paul's calling (Acts 9:15-16). He is simply stating that his ministry is from God because it is characterized by suffering. Note the following cross references:

From henceforth let no man trouble me: for I bear in my body the marks of the Lord Jesus. (Gal. 6:17)

That I may know him, and the power of his resurrection, and the fellowship of his sufferings, being made conformable unto his death. (Phil. 3:10)

Howbeit for this cause I obtained mercy, that in me first Jesus Christ might shew forth all longsuffering, for a pattern to them which should hereafter believe on him to life everlasting. (1 Tim. 1:16)

"For his body's sake, which is the church" proves again that the word church can be used to designate the body of all believers, not just the local body of believers. Those who embrace the faulty *Baptist Bride* position would do well to recognize a few things:

1. A local assembly (church) can contain unsaved members, whereas the "church which is his body" consists only of saved people.
2. Local assemblies are plural in number, but the body of Christ is singular ("one body" – Eph. 4:4).
3. Unassembled believers are called a church (Acts 8:3, 12:5).
4. Paul includes himself in the same body he wrote to (Rom. 12:5; 1 Cor. 12:13 and Eph. 5:30).
5. All saved people in this age are included in the bride or their names are not in the book of life (Rev. 21:27).
6. "In Christ" doesn't refer to church membership by water baptism, but salvation by spirit baptism (Gal. 3:26-28).

"Whereof I am made a minister." Paul was never ashamed of his calling and apostleship. He was the apostle and minister to the Gentiles (Rom. 11:13; 15:16-19). Although he didn't replace Judas as one of the twelve (see Acts 1:26), he was the author of a large portion of the New

Testament and received the revelation of the mystery of the body of Christ.

"According to the dispensation of God." Here the word dispensation is used for the fourth time in the Bible (the others are 1 Cor. 9:17; Eph. 1:10; 3:2), and it is clear from the context that the word does *not* mean "a period of time." Because for many years' authors have referred to it as such, people often assume "a period of time" is the correct definition. The English definition (from *The Random House College Dictionary*, 382) is as follows:

1. The act or an instance of dispensing; distribution.

2. Something that is distributed or given out.

3. A specified order, system, or arrangement; administration or management.

Paul is stating that he is a minister not by his own will or conviction (see Gal. 1:16) but that he is following the order and arrangement of God's will to fulfill his calling. Paul was giving out (dispensing) what God told him to give out (dispense). As the minister and apostle to the Gentiles, Paul was given certain revelations concerning this *age* of the church that the other apostles were not given.

---

26 *Even* the mystery which hath been hid from ages and from generations, but now is made manifest to his saints:

27 To whom God would make known what *is* the riches of the glory of this mystery among the Gentiles; which is Christ in you, the hope of glory:

Paul's revelation of the **"mystery"** in verse twenty-six is defined in verse twenty-seven as **"Christ in you, the hope of glory."** While John alluded to this when quoting Christ (John 14:17, 20) it was not taught in this fashion until God revealed it to Paul.

This mystery is referred to as the mystery of the body of Christ and teaches that upon conversion all believers are spiritually baptized (Rom. 6:1-4) into the body of Jesus Christ. Christ is inside of the believer's body, and believers are inside of Christ.

Jesus dwelled inside of believers *prior* to Paul receiving revelation concerning this mystery. Hyper-dispensationalists teach that the body of Christ did not begin until *after* Paul's conversion. But this is not biblical. Paul was the first to *know* about this mystery, but just because a thing is not *known* does not mean it does not *exist*. Paul even stated there were others "in Christ" before he was saved, plus the book of Acts verifies the truth of the "one body" *prior* to Paul's salvation:

Salute Andronicus and Junia, my kinsmen, and my fellowprisoners, who are of note among the apostles, who also were in Christ before me. (Rom. 16:7)

And believers were the more added to the Lord, multitudes both of men and women. (Acts 5:14)

This mystery of **"Christ in you"** was **"hid from ages and from generations."** The Old Testament does not reveal it, nor do any other authors in the New Testament (except for those partial inferences by John). When Paul refers to "the mystery of the gospel" (Eph. 6:19), he's including this mystery as well as the mystery of the rapture of the church (1 Thess. 4:13-18; 1 Cor. 15:51-57). These are the reasons why Paul called the gospel that he preached "his gospel" (Rom. 2:16; 16:25; 2 Tim. 2:8).

"Among the Gentiles." Paul doesn't mention the Gentiles because only Gentiles compose the body of Christ. We know this is *not* the case (see Eph. 2:11-19). He mentions Gentiles because he is the apostle to the Gentiles (Rom. 11:13; 15:16-19) and most believers at the church in Colosse were Gentiles. Paul reveals this mystery to those to whom he was sent.

"The hope of glory" is Jesus Christ inside of us. There is no hope in our flesh. There is no hope in our fellow man. As the old hymn says:

> My hope is built on nothing less
> Than Jesus blood and righteousness.

And while the Holy Spirit came inside believers in the Old Testament (Gen. 41:38; Ex. 28:3; Num. 27:18; 1 Peter 1:11; Dan. 4:8; 6:3; Isa. 63:11), He didn't indwell them *permanently* in the same manner that He does *after* Calvary.

> He that believeth on me, as the scripture hath said, out of his belly shall flow rivers of living water. (But this spake he of the Spirit, which they that believe on him should receive: for the Holy Ghost was not yet given; because that Jesus was not yet glorified.) (John 7:38-39)

The Holy Spirit was not "given" in the same sense in the Old Testament. There was no *permanent* indwelling of the risen Christ in saints *before* the cross. The Spirit could come and go. Notice David's prayer after he sinned:

> Cast me not away from thy presence; and take not thy holy spirit from me. (Ps. 51:11)

Notice also what happened to Saul and Samson:

> But the Spirit of the LORD departed from Saul, and an evil spirit from the LORD troubled him. (1 Sam. 16:14)

And she said, The Philistines be upon thee, Samson. And he awoke out of his sleep, and said, I will go out as at other times before, and shake myself. And he wist not that the LORD was departed from him. (Judg. 16:20)

When a person gets saved in this age (after Calvary) the Spirit of God comes inside of them to dwell forever. Jesus spoke of this in John 14:16, and Paul explained this as a "sealing work" in Ephesians:

In whom ye also trusted, after that ye heard the word of truth, the gospel of your salvation: in whom also after that ye believed, ye were sealed with that holy Spirit of promise. (Eph. 1:13)

And grieve not the holy Spirit of God, whereby ye are sealed unto the day of redemption. (Eph. 4:30)

---

28 Whom we preach, warning every man, and teaching every man in all wisdom; that we may present every man perfect in Christ Jesus:
29 Whereunto I also labour, striving according to his working, which worketh in me mightily.

"Whom we preach." Although Paul did *teach* great spiritual truths, he was mainly a *preacher*. Notice that we can't find Paul preaching:

1. Politics.
2. Social programs.
3. Psychology.
4. Philosophy.
5. Constitutional reformations.
6. Marriage seminars.

Paul preached Jesus Christ and Him alone. Jesus is enough. Pastor, if people don't want to come to church to hear preaching about Jesus, then you don't need them weighing down your pews!

"Warning every man." This mystery has a practical side to it. It isn't just all philosophical ideals but rather practical help for daily living. In other words, if Jesus Christ is in you, He should change the way you live.

"Teaching every man in all wisdom" means there should be teaching along with the preaching. Jesus not only preached, but He also taught the people (Mark 12:35; John 7:14). **"In all wisdom."** Paul gave individual attention when it was needed, and he also was aware of whom he was teaching. He used wisdom and discretion in how he approached and taught different people. The Lord told the disciples to be "wise as serpents, and harmless as doves" (Matt. 10:16).

"Present every man perfect in Christ Jesus." This *perfection* has to do with our walk with God – doing what we know to do, to the best of our ability (Phil. 3:12-15). It is not saying that a Christian can be sinless. You will continue to sin until your death or the rapture.

Paul's goal was that those to whom he preached be right with the Lord and presentable to the Lord when He called them home. To this end he **"laboured,"** not by his own strength, but according to the power of God which worked in him **"mightily."**

COLOSSIANS CHAPTER 2

---

1 For I would that ye knew what great conflict I have for you, and *for* them at Laodicea, and *for* as many as have not seen my face in the flesh;

2 That their hearts might be comforted, being knit together in love, and unto all riches of the full assurance of understanding, to the acknowledgement of the mystery of God, and of the Father, and of Christ;

3 In whom are hid all the treasures of wisdom and knowledge.

Paul's **"conflict"** relates to his personal burden for the spiritual welfare of the Colossians and other churches that he was not able to visit personally. As Phillips stated (page 98), the problem in Laodicea was *luxury,* while in Colosse it was *lies.* Here, in a roundabout way, Paul was rebuking Gnostic teachings – their misunderstandings of the true mysteries which are found *only* in Christ.

"Hearts might be comforted...full assurance." One of the greatest proofs for correct doctrine is found in what it produces. Greek philosophy and Gnosticism do not give lasting comfort or assurance. True comfort comes only from the Bible and the Lord Jesus (see Rom. 15:4; 2 Cor. 1:3; Phil. 2:1; 1 Thess. 4:18).

"Full assurance" is something that religions cannot give because all they offer are "hope so's" or "maybes." Religious interpretation leaves the sinner hopeless while biblical salvation leaves him with assurance of what God did!

These things have I written unto you that believe on the name of the Son of God; that ye may know that ye have eternal life, and that ye may believe on the name of the Son of God. (1 John 5:13)

"The mystery of God" is mentioned in Revelation 10:7 and relates to God's plan and program for getting the title deed of the earth back under His domain. The **"mystery...of the Father"** perhaps relates to the incarnation of the Father in the Son (Isa. 9:6; Matt. 1:23; 1 Tim. 3:16). The **"mystery...of Christ"** shows that both Jews and Gentiles are part of the same body of believers in this age (Eph. 3:4-6).

Verse three condemns Gnosticism by stating that wisdom and knowledge come only *through* the Lord Jesus Christ, not by just *using* Him or knowing *about* Him. The **"treasures of wisdom and knowledge"** are **"in"** Christ. It is Jesus Christ that can open the eyes of our understanding to the scriptures (Luke 24:32-45).

Therefore, anyone who attempts to find wisdom by any other means will fail and be deceived! Occasional truths in philosophy only verify the Devil's tactics. Seventy-five percent of what Satan told Eve was *true*. The wisdom of this world will always deceive and damn because it is contrary to God and His word. Notice God's commentary:

For it is written, I will destroy the wisdom of the wise, and will bring to nothing the understanding of the prudent. Where is the wise? where is the scribe? where is the disputer of this world? hath not God made foolish the wisdom of this world? (1 Cor. 1:19-20)

But of him are ye in Christ Jesus, who of God is made unto us wisdom, and righteousness, and sanctification, and redemption. (1 Cor. 1:30)

That your faith should not stand in the wisdom of men, but in the power of God. (1 Cor. 2:5)

Which things also we speak, not in the words which man's wisdom teacheth, but which the Holy Ghost teacheth; comparing spiritual things with spiritual. (1 Cor. 2:13)

The world is empty of *real* wisdom. Solomon proved this point in the book of Ecclesiastes when he discussed life from man's point of view. Without God and the Bible, man has a purposeless existence. Fun and pleasure will not fill the void of man's heart:

I said in mine heart, Go to now, I will prove thee with mirth, therefore enjoy pleasure: and, behold, this also is vanity. (Eccl. 2:1)

Solomon came up empty when he tried to find comfort and happiness in pleasure alone ("this also is vanity"). Real wisdom and knowledge are found in knowing the One who *is* wisdom and knowledge (1 Cor. 1:30). Only with *Him* will you find what you are missing – God's own presence. Man, without God is a miserable wreck. He is endlessly trying to find happiness in pleasure. But like Solomon, man's appetite will never be filled until it is finally full of God Himself.

---

4 And this I say, lest any man should beguile you with enticing words.

5 For though I be absent in the flesh, yet am I with you in the spirit, joying and beholding your order, and the stedfastness of your faith in Christ.

"Any man" could certainly include a religious shyster who *uses* the Bible and claims to follow the Lord.

"Enticing words" would include words that flatter you with praise or seduce you with covetousness. Watch out for those who always pat you on the back because the other hand my hold a knife!

Paul's preaching and teaching to the Colossians was different from the Gnostics, not only by the *truth* he preached, but by *how* he preached the truth. The Gnostics so-called facts were actually lies or partial truth laced with lies (Gal. 5:9). Paul, on the other hand, was teaching God's pure truth without admixture of error.

In addition, the Gnostics taught with enticing and positive words of man's philosophy (verse eight) – words that would appeal to the natural man in an attempt to beguile him.

Paul, however, preached the truth "straight from the hip and over the plate, waist high" so the people had no trouble understanding him:

> And my speech and my preaching was not with enticing words of man's wisdom, but in demonstration of the Spirit and of power: That your faith should not stand in the wisdom of men, but in the power of God. (1 Cor. 2:4-5)

> For neither at any time used we flattering words, as ye know, nor a cloke of covetousness; God is witness. (1 Thess. 2:5)

The Bible describes these deceivers who are so positive and loving in their speech:

> For they that are such serve not our Lord Jesus Christ, but their own belly; and by good words and fair speeches deceive the hearts of the simple. (Rom. 16:18)

Paul was warning them not to listen to smooth talkers. He implied that even though he was not with them **"in the flesh"** (verse one) he was still with them **"in the spirit"** and knew what was going on in their assembly (verse five).

---

6 As ye have therefore received Christ Jesus the Lord, *so* walk ye in him:

7 Rooted and built up in him, and stablished in the faith, as ye have been taught, abounding therein with thanksgiving.

When Paul said, **"and this I say"** (verse four), he prefaced it with verse five. In other words, he was saying, "You'd better be careful because I know what is going on there!" He then proceeded to command them to remember their *past* salvation so they might live right in the *present* (verse six).

"As ye have therefore received Christ." How does anyone receive Christ? By faith. Although saved by faith, the Colossians had quit walking by faith and were now walking by sight and the teachings of the world. Paul rebukes the Galatians similarly:

> This only would I learn of you, Received ye the Spirit by the works of the law, or by the hearing of faith? Are ye so foolish? having begun in the Spirit, are ye now made perfect by the flesh? (Gal. 3:2-3)

You are to walk (or live) by faith just as you were saved by faith. And since you have believed in Christ to save your soul, you should also believe in Christ to direct your life and your works. *Walking* and *working* according to your own sight is the opposite of trusting the Lord to guide you. Why would a Christian, who knows he was saved by faith without works, attempt to justify himself before God through his works?

"Rooted and built up in him." The root or foundation must be Jesus Christ (1 Cor. 3:11). Any other foundation is shifting sand. Verse seven lists some basic truths for new believers:

1. You must be saved, rooted in Christ (Rev. 5:5).
2. You must allow this root to grow – to be **"built up"** (2 Peter 3:18).
3. You must be **"in the faith"** – established in good solid Bible doctrine.

4. You must continue to learn **"as ye have been taught"** from good teachers of the word of God.

5. You should always have an attitude of **"thanksgiving,"** remembering what God has done for you.

---

8 Beware lest any man spoil you through philosophy and vain deceit, after the tradition of men, after the rudiments of the world, and not after Christ.

Verse eight warns a Christian to **"beware"** of letting those things listed happen to him. A careless Christian could become unaware of the deceit in man's philosophy and thus become:

1. Spoiled.
2. Deceived.
3. Worldly.
4. Tradition followers instead of Christ's followers.

"Any man" includes worldly philosophers, Gnostics, or even Christian pastors who have been schooled by an apostate seminary.

According to Webster's 1828 dictionary, "spoil" means:

1. To pull asunder, to tear, to strip, to peel.
2. To plunder; to strip by violence; to rob; as, to spoil one of his goods or possessions.
3. To seize by violence; to take by force; as, to spoil one's goods.
4. To corrupt; to cause to decay and perish.
5. To ruin; to destroy. Our crops are sometimes spoiled by insects.

The warning is clear. Your spiritual life can be destroyed and plundered if you take heed to the philosophical systems of man. The Oprah's and Dr. Phil's of this world are eager to instruct you in their worldly carnal beliefs. And even though they may teach *some* truth, the "whole lump" is still a deceitful lie (1 Cor. 5:6; Gal. 5:9).

"Through philosophy." This is the only occurrence of the word **"philosophy"** in the Bible. *Philosophy* means "a lover of wisdom." But in the scripture, we are told to love God first (Matt. 22:37-38), not wisdom. We are also told that true wisdom comes from God alone (Prov. 2:6) never from man's own understanding (Prov. 3:5-6). God is unimpressed with man's wisdom:

> Where is the wise? where is the scribe? where is the disputer of this world? hath not God made foolish the wisdom of this world? For after that in the wisdom of God the world by wisdom knew not God, it pleased God by the foolishness of preaching to save them that believe. (1 Cor. 1:20-21)

The philosophical systems of today can be categorized into the four major areas. Dr. Ruckman (*The Christian's Handbook of Science and Philosophy*, pages 15-20) defines and classifies these areas as:

1. Naturalism – reality that can be perceived by the five senses (taste, seeing, touch, smelling and hearing).
2. Idealism – the ultimate reality is not the physical but the ideals that you believe in.
3. Realism – a joining of naturalism and idealism.
4. Pragmatism – dealing only with application. Whatever gets the job done, whatever works, is considered good. The end justifies the means.

All these philosophies have four things in common that help the Christian both identify and avoid them.

1. They are **"vain."** Solomon declared all the different philosophical views as "vanity of vanities" (Eccl. 1:2).

2. They are *deceitful* **("vain deceit").** Their purpose is to lure the unaware Christian away from God and His truths.

3. They are based on the **"tradition[s] of men"** rather than the word of God.

4. They are founded on **the "rudiments of the world, and not after Christ."**

Those four truths are basic. You don't have to know everything about all belief systems to know that they are wrong (see Prov. 18:1).

1. Philosophy is vain because it presents no clear absolute revelation of untarnished truth.

2. Philosophy is deceitful because it cannot deliver what it promises. It gives no assurance of anything, including life after death.

3. Philosophy is after man's traditions and depraved perceptions. Developed without God and His truth, philosophy is twisted and perverted (Mark 7:9)

4. Philosophy appeals to the flesh instead of the spirit because it is carnal and worldly. Moreover, it is contrary to the Lord and His written revelation.

"After the rudiments of the world." The unsaved man who is blind to God's revelation of truth generates these philosophies naturally (1 Cor. 2:14; 2 Cor. 4:4). They are all he has. Consequently, these false ideas spring up not just on college campuses, but also on farms, mechanic shops, and all other places unsaved men may be. Lost people everywhere espouse false beliefs without even knowing the specific name of the philosophy. If you spend time talking to people about the Lord and salvation, you will uncover a myriad of false beliefs that are contrary to the truth **"and not after Christ."**

The best way to counter these false ideas is with scripture and a clear presentation of the gospel of Jesus Christ. Don't become entrapped on their playing field by trying to disprove a certain philosophy. Simply present the truth of the gospel and what the scriptures say. If the Bible cannot convince them, you can't convince them!

---

9 For in him dwelleth all the fulness of the Godhead bodily.

The **"in him,"** of course, refers back to the **"Christ"** of verse eight.

Verse nine teaches us that everything we need to know about God and His wisdom is found in Jesus Christ. As the song says, "I found it all in Jesus, my searching is through; all things are new. I found it all in Jesus and you can find Him, too."

"Godhead bodily." That the word Godhead is found in scripture three times is appropriate because it refers to the triune nature of God. See Acts 17:29; Rom. 1:20 and here, Col. 2:9. The Bible word for Trinity is Godhead.

The teaching of the Trinity is antithetical to the teaching of polytheism which is a belief in many (i.e., poly-) gods. Polytheism (according to Cloud's *Way of Life Encyclopedia* page 579) differs from Christianity in these ways:

1. Their gods are many while the true God is One. Hindu gods, for instance, fight one another, marry one another, create one another, and destroy one another.

2. Their gods are revealed in many manifestations. In contrast, the Bible teaches that God is revealed in one manifestation – the incarnation of God in the person of the Lord Jesus Christ.

3. Their gods hold different degrees of deity while the three Persons of the Trinity are equal.

Tri-theism which teaches that there are actually three separate gods and Unitarianism which teaches there is one God who manifests power in different ways are two other systems that deny the biblical Trinity.

The two most prevalent heresies regarding the doctrine of the Trinity are these:

1. Arianism (from Aruis A.D. 300) teaches that the Father is God, but that Jesus Christ is a *begotten* god, and the Holy Spirit is only a force. The modern-day cult of the Jehovah's Witnesses believes this heresy (supported by the NASB in John 1:18). They reason that the Father and the Son are unequal since they are different.

2. Sabellianism (from Sabellius A.D. 250), on the other hand, teaches that since the Father and Son are both equal that there is no difference at all. Their modern-day representatives would be the "Jesus Only" groups.

The problem people have with the Trinity is not so much that it contradicts the scriptures but that it contradicts the human mind. Chafer (274) said, "No argument has been advanced against the Trinitarian conception other than that it does not conform to the limitations of the mind of man." And as Tozer rightly stated (*Knowledge of the Holy* page 23):

> The doctrine of the Trinity is truth for the heart. The fact that it cannot be satisfactorily explained, instead of being against it, is in its favor. Such a truth had to be revealed; no one could have imagined it.

Below are a few Bible proofs for the doctrine of the Trinity:

1. All three (Father, Son and Holy Ghost) are called God (Col. 1:2; John 1:1; Acts 5:3, 4; 2 Cor. 3:17).
2. All three have divine attributes:
   a. Holiness (John 17:11; Acts 3:14; Eph. 4:30)
   b. Omnipotence (1 Peter 1:5; Matt. 28:18; Rom. 15:19)
   c. Omniscience (Rom. 11:33; John 21:17; 1 Cor. 2:11)
   d. Omnipresence (Jer. 23:24; Matt. 18:20; Ps. 139:7)
   e. Eternal (1 Tim. 1:17; John 1:1; Heb. 9:14)
3. All three perform divine works:
   a. Creation (Gen. 1:1; John 1:3; Gen. 1:2)
   b. Salvation (Eph. 1:6; Rev. 3:20; Titus 3:5)
   c. Security (1 Peter 1:5; Jude 1; Eph. 1:13)

"Godhead bodily." Jesus clarified the teaching when He spoke with Phillip. Earlier the Lord had taught that no one but Himself had ever seen God the Father:

> No man hath seen God at any time; the only begotten Son, which is in the bosom of the Father, he hath declared him. (John 1:18)
> Not that any man hath seen the Father, save he which is of God, he hath seen the Father. (John 6:46)

But prior to the crucifixion, the Lord taught plainly and emphatically that He was indeed equal with God and the actual body of God Himself – "God was manifest in the flesh..." (1 Tim. 3:16):

> I and my Father are one. Then the Jews took up stones again to stone him. Jesus answered them, Many good works have I shewed you from my Father; for which of those works do ye stone me? The Jews answered him, saying, For a good work we stone thee not; but for blasphemy; and because that thou, being a man, makest thyself God. (John 10:30-33)

> Jesus saith unto him, Have I been so long time with you, and yet hast thou not known me, Philip? he that hath seen me hath seen the Father; and how sayest thou then, Shew us the Father? (John 14:9)

Since God is a triune being, and since we were created in His image, God can be identified as

1. God the Father – the soul or essence of God. The soul is the part of God and man that no one can see (John 1:18).
2. God the Son – the body of God. Jesus had a physical body of flesh, bone, and blood just as all men do.
3. God the Holy Spirit – the Spirit of God which cannot be seen as the Son was but can indeed be felt (unlike the Father).

We see this marvelously illustrated in the creation of Adam:

> And the very God of peace sanctify you wholly; and I pray God your whole spirit and soul and body be preserved blameless unto the coming of our Lord Jesus Christ. (1 Thess. 5:23)

> And the LORD God formed man of the dust of the ground, and breathed into his nostrils the breath of life; and man became a living soul. (Gen. 2:7)

1. The body – "formed man of the dust of the ground..."

2. The spirit – "the breath of life..."

3. The soul – "man became a living soul."

---

10 And ye are complete in him, which is the head of all principality and power:

Verse ten makes the doctrine of the Trinity practical and relevant. Our worth or self-esteem is not based on our personal value which is "less than nothing, and vanity" (Isa. 40:17) but rather on Christ. In Him we are **"complete"** (verse ten) and can be who God wants us to be.

Jesus Christ is the **"head of all principality and power"** which means that He has complete control over all powers in the universe (Matt. 28:28; Col. 1:16). In Him we are not only complete but also "more than conquerors through him that loved us" (Rom. 8:37).

---

11 In whom also ye are circumcised with the circumcision made without hands, in putting off the body of the sins of the flesh by the circumcision of Christ:

12 Buried with him in baptism, wherein also ye are risen with *him* through the faith of the operation of God, who hath raised him from the dead.

13 And you, being dead in your sins and the uncircumcision of your flesh, hath he quickened together with him, having forgiven you all trespasses;

"In whom" refers back to Christ. The blessings that we have as Christians stem from the fact that we are in Jesus Christ, reaping His benefits. There is no hint of personal merit. It is all grace!

"Circumcised with the circumcision made without hands." This is **"the circumcision of Christ"** which is a literal operation that takes place inside every person who trusts Jesus Christ as his personal Saviour. Notice:

1. A circumcising is a cutting.

2. It is called **"the circumcision of Christ"** because Jesus Christ Himself performs it.

3. This cutting is **"made without hands."** In other words, it is not a physical operation but rather a spiritual **"operation of God"** (verse twelve).

4. This cutting separates the **"sins of the flesh"** from soul and spirit of the believer. Note that before a person is saved, the soul is equated to the flesh because the sins of the flesh also corrupt the soul (Lev. 7:18; Num. 15:28; Ezek. 18:4, 20; John 8:21-24; Eph. 2:1).

5. The operation without hands is performed by the word of God:

> For the word of God is quick, and powerful, and sharper than any twoedged sword, piercing even to the dividing asunder of soul and spirit, and of the joints and marrow, and is a discerner of the thoughts and intents of the heart. (Heb. 4:12)

6. Once the soul and spirit are separated from the "joints and marrow," the sins of the flesh cannot corrupt the soul, thereby securing its eternal salvation and leaving every believer with two distinct natures. Because the flesh and the spirit are no longer joined, they do constant battle (Gal. 5:17).

7. This operation places the new creature into Jesus Christ by a burial that is called a baptism. See Rom. 6:1-4 and Eph. 4:4-6.

8. With this operation, there is also a simultaneous spiritual resurrection (verse twelve) that identifies the believer with the resurrection of Jesus Christ. This resurrection gives life or "quickens" the child of God (verse thirteen with Eph. 2:1-2), assuring him that he has been forgiven all **"trespasses"** (verse thirteen).

The doctrinal implication of verses 11-13 is great. For they categorically teach the absolute safety and eternal security of the child of God. A person dies and goes to hell because sin is on his soul. When a person believes on Christ for salvation, the **"sins of flesh"** are separated from the soul. The soul is saved, and the spirit is "born again" (John 3:3-5). The Holy Spirit seals the believer so that the sins of the old man (or the flesh) cannot affect the new man inside. Furthermore, the Christian's old life is dead and buried while the new man is alive and resurrected. 1 John 3:9 can finally be reconciled:

> Whosoever is born of God doth not commit sin; for his seed remaineth in him: and he cannot sin, because he is born of God. (1 John 3:9)

Your flesh was not born of God, it was born of man. But when you received Christ, your spirit was born again, and your soul saved. It cannot sin because you have been operated on. The flesh is separated from the spirit and soul so that the sins of the flesh cannot stain and pollute your soul. You are in Jesus Christ – not your flesh but your spirit (1 Cor. 6:17).

This verse establishes our doctrine as well as helping us practically. Since we have been circumcised spiritually with our sins no longer affecting our eternal destiny, we can have the full assurance that we are **"forgiven"** of **"all trespasses."** Many Christians never comprehend this blessed truth. They continually anguish over their past sins. If you are saved, you have been forgiven; you have been cleared. You have a new life in Christ and can live triumphantly by His resurrection power (Rom. 8:11).

---

14 Blotting out the handwriting of ordinances that was against us, which was contrary to us, and took it out of the way, nailing it to his cross;

15 *And* having spoiled principalities and powers, he made a shew of them openly, triumphing over them in it.

Verses 14 and 15 happened at the death, burial, and resurrection of our Lord. **"Blotting out"** means doing away with (compare with Ex. 32:32, 33; Num. 5:23; Deut 9:14; 25:19; 29:20). Jesus blotted out the **"ordinances"** which have to do with the commandments and ceremonial observances found in the Mosaic Law.

"Against us, which was contrary to us." The laws and observances were against man, not in his favor. Sinless obedience to a holy God was absolutely impossible. But while people did "keep" the Old Testament Law (see Josh. 22:2; Judg. 2:17; 1 Kings 11:34; Luke 1:6) they still never had their sins taken away or cleared by the law.

> For it is not possible that the blood of bulls and of goats should take away sins. (Heb. 10:4)

"Took it out of the way, nailing it to his cross." So, the rituals, ceremonies, and laws (including the Sabbath – verse sixteen) are not in force to be observed anymore. When Jesus died, the law was fulfilled finally and forever. The final sacrifice was made for sin, and a new covenant was instituted (Matt. 26:28). The early church struggled with this because they were all Jews, and the Law was an integral part of their society and culture. In the book of Acts, you will notice that after the resurrection, this truth was revealed progressively rather than directly. In Acts 15 the disciples understood that neither salvation nor sanctification was connected with the ordinances. They wrote to the Gentiles telling them that observance of Jewish customs was not required.

"And having spoiled principalities and powers." When the Lord Jesus went to the cross there was a spiritual battle raging that no one in the flesh could see. Satan and his hosts of devils were no doubt assailing the Lord. Satan had begun even earlier when the Lord went to the garden of Gethsemane (see Matt. 16:23). The Bible records a glimpse of what was going on behind the scenes:

> The Lord GOD hath opened mine ear, and I was not rebellious, neither turned away back. I gave my back to the smiters, and my cheeks to them that plucked off the hair: I hid not my face from shame and spitting. For the Lord GOD will help me; therefore shall I not be confounded: therefore have I set my face like a flint, and I know that I shall not be ashamed. He is near that justifieth me; who will contend with me? let us stand together: who is mine adversary? let him come near to me. (Isa. 50:5-8)

The above reference includes the Father ("The Lord GOD"), the Son ("I gave my back to the smiters") and Satan ("who is mine adversary?").

Our Lord won the battle! Death could not keep Him. He returned to His Father's house with the "keys of hell and of death" (Rev. 1:18). He not only defeated Satan and the evil powers, but He also **"spoiled"** them! The very thing meant to destroy Him (the cross) became His mighty weapon against the foe. The **"it"** (end of verse fifteen) must refer to the cross!

In view of the victory of Christ, Paul goes on to make practical application:

---

16 Let no man therefore judge you in meat, or in drink, or in respect of an holyday, or of the new moon, or of the sabbath *days*:

17 Which are a shadow of things to come; but the body is of Christ.

"Therefore" refers back to verses 14-15. Since the ordinances were crucified with Christ, and since Christ was triumphant in the battle, we shouldn't let anyone attempt to bring us back into captivity of these things which Christ did away with in verse sixteen.

The laws regarding **"meat, or in drink"** can be found in Lev. 11 and Deut. 14. But in this age, Paul equates the forcing of dietary laws to demon possession:

> Now the Spirit speaketh expressly, that in the latter times some shall depart from the faith, giving heed to seducing spirits, and doctrines of devils; Speaking lies in hypocrisy; having their conscience seared with a hot iron; Forbidding to marry, and commanding to abstain from meats, which God hath created to be received with thanksgiving of them which believe and know the truth. For every creature of God is good, and nothing to be refused, if it be received with thanksgiving: For it is sanctified by the word of God and prayer. (1 Tim. 4:1-5)

Now, obviously the sin of gluttony (eating in excess) is still a sin because it abuses the Christian's body which belongs to God (1 Cor. 6:19, 20). But in this age, there is no *spiritual value* to abstaining from certain types of foods. Of course, there may be some specific physical value relating to individual health (e.g., a diabetic's diet), but there is no binding order from God stating that a New Testament Christian must only eat and drink specific things. Should you watch what you eat? Should you take care of the body God has given you? Absolutely! But don't connects physical health with spirituality. The Colossians were tangled in this very snare (see verses 21-23).

"Sabbath days." Back then there were some apostate Jews trying to force Sabbath observance on the Colossians. Today, Seventh Day Adventists try to convince Christians that we should meet on Saturday instead of Sunday. Below are some Bible truths about the Sabbath:

1. Adam, Noah, and Abraham never revered the seventh day as holy. It wasn't revealed as a special day until God spoke to Moses on Mount Sinai (Ezek. 20:12, 20; Neh. 9:14).

2. The Sabbath and its multiple days of observance (see Lev. 23:5-7, 24; Num. 28:16-18) were given to the Jews as a SIGN: Ex. 16:23 20:8-11; 31:12-17.

3. The Sabbath is considered in both the moral and ceremonial law. See: Lev. 19:3 and Ex. 20:8.

4. The moral law and the ceremonial law are both replaced for the Christian: John 15:10-12; Rom. 13:9-11; 2 Cor. 3:6, 7.

5. Jesus Christ arose on the first day of the week (John 20:1); the Holy Spirit descended on the first day of the week (Acts 2:1); Christians assembled with each other on the first day of the week (Acts 20:6-7); Paul taught this to the early churches (2 Cor. 16:1-2).

6. Just because there were cases where Christian preachers went into a synagogue on Saturday to preach to unsaved Jews does not mean that Christians are to gather on Saturday. They were simply evangelizing wherever and whenever they could, even to assemblies on the Sabbath.

"Which are a shadow of things to come." In other words, some Jewish ordinances including Sabbath days will be instituted again in the future. Note:

> And it shall come to pass, that from one new moon to another, and from one sabbath to another, shall all flesh come to worship before me, saith the LORD. (Isa. 66:23)

In Ezekiel 40-48 we read that temple observance for Jews will be reinstated in the millennium. The New Covenant is a blessing of forgiveness for the nation of Israel (Jer. 31:31-33). National atonement is granted to the nation based on Levitical animal sacrifices. These sacrifices are not for individuals, but for the nation. The following scriptures highlight the blotting out of Israel's sins at the Second Advent see: Ps. 85:2; Isa. 4:4; 33:24; 40:2; 43:25; Jer. 50:10; Ezek. 45:15; Mic. 7:18; Zech. 3:9; Acts 3:19; Rom. 11:26-28.

Dr. Ruckman (in his book *How to Teach Dispensational Truth*) rightly stated that "every theological lie in this age is a biblical truth misplaced." There are cults teaching things for today that have application for the future age. They fail to make the proper divisions in scripture (2 Tim. 2:15) so the two-edged sword (Heb. 4:12) slices them to pieces.

---

18 Let no man beguile you of your reward in a voluntary humility and worshipping of angels, intruding into those things which he hath not seen, vainly puffed up by his fleshly mind,

19 And not holding the Head, from which all the body by joints and bands having nourishment ministered, and knit together, increaseth with the increase of God.

Earlier Paul warned about being beguiled with **"enticing words"** (verse four). Then he told us to **"beware"** of philosophy. Now he exhorts us to be careful not to lose our reward by following these super pious, angel worshipping, carnal deceivers. To be *beguiled* out of our reward implies we may lose rewards at the Judgment Seat of Christ:

> Look to yourselves, that we lose not those things which we have wrought, but that we receive a full reward. (2 John 8)

The characteristics of these deceivers are listed as follows:

1. They are vain.

2. They are carnally minded instead of heavenly minded.

3. They are proud **("puffed up").**

4. They worship angels instead of God (see Rev. 19:10).

"Not holding the Head." These false teachers propagate their heretical garbage because they do not regard the Lord Jesus Christ as the Head. They fail to give Him the preeminence (Col. 1:18).

---

20 Wherefore if ye be dead with Christ from the rudiments of the world, why, as though living in the world, are ye subject to ordinances,

21(Touch not; taste not; handle not;

22 Which all are to perish with the using;) after the commandments and doctrines of men?

23 Which things have indeed a shew of wisdom in will worship, and humility, and neglecting of the body; not in any honour to the satisfying of the flesh.

"Subject to ordinances." This phrase would have application to any list of rules or standards that a religious organization may try to implement. As Phillips said (page 150) "The New Testament deals in principles, not lists of rules." Unfortunately, some pastors and churches try to uphold a standard of whatever they deem to be spiritual. Many of these standards are not Christian at all. For if you tried to initiate them on the mission field or in a nursing home, you would be quickly forced to *bend* the rules.

The summary is as follows:

1. If you are dead with Christ, then you should be dead to the carnal influences of the world.

2. Since the old man is dead, you should not follow petty laws concerning works of the flesh (**"touch not; taste not; handle not"**).

3. These **"doctrines of men"** (verse twenty-two) are not from God and don't produce spirituality.

4. The **"wisdom"** and **"will worship, and humility"** (verse twenty-three) are only for an outward **"shew"** and are of no real profit for a Christian.

Phillips (153) rightly summarizes:

The whole cultic system with its boasted secret knowledge, its abuse of the body, its "will worship," its imposition of iron discipline, its strict adherence to rules and regulations, and its fascination with religious codes, whether those of the eastern guru or those of the western monk, does no good. God rejects it. And, in the end, the flesh is still there as fierce, as strong, and as wicked as ever.

COLOSSIANS CHAPTER 3

---

1 If ye then be risen with Christ, seek those things which are above, where Christ sitteth on the right hand of God.

2 Set your affection on things above, not on things on the earth.

3 For ye are dead, and your life is hid with Christ in God.

4 When Christ, *who* is our life, shall appear, then shall ye also appear with him in glory.

Paul did not doubt that the Colossians were saved. Rather he uses the phrase **"if ye"** as we would use the word "since." Notice how he uses this phrase elsewhere:

> And if ye be Christ's, then are ye Abraham's seed, and heirs according to the promise. (Gal. 3:29)

> Wherefore if ye be dead with Christ from the rudiments of the world, why, as though living in the world, are ye subject to ordinances. (Col. 2:20)

Paul states a practical truth: "Since you belong to Christ and are identified with Him in death, burial and resurrection, you should desire eternal things instead of earthly things."

"Risen with Christ." Not only is the Christian "crucified with Christ" (Gal. 2:20) and "buried with him" (Rom. 6:4) he is also risen with Christ to a new life (2 Cor. 5:17). Eternal life, as well as new life in Christ, is a present possession for a Christian. If you are saved, your old life is dead and buried. The Lord has forgiven all your sins, so you have a brand-new life. Here Paul gives details about how to live this new life according to God's will.

"Seek those things which are above." One day Jesus asked two of John's disciples, "What seek ye?" (John 1:38) and here He answers that question – **"things which are above."** Some think you can be so heavenly minded that you are no earthly good, but in reality, if you are not heavenly minded you won't be any earthly good! What are you seeking in your life? Are you seeking after things that are eternal, or after things that are material and temporal, like cars, houses, jobs or relationships? Check yourself to see if you are truly seeking the right things.

"Seek those things which are above." The things which are above would include

1. New Jerusalem.
2. Eternal rewards.
3. God's face.
4. God's throne.
5. Jesus Christ.

Our hearts should be turned toward heaven and not this earth. Notice verse two:

"Set your affection on things above, not on things on the earth." The KJV's translation of "froneite" as "affection" is much more accurate than the word "mind" which is found in the new versions. The word "affection" speaks of the heart motives as well as the intellectual processes.

We are to have a heart for God and the things of God. We are to love what God loves instead of things on this earth. The following steps may help in keeping a heavenly perspective:

1. Believe what God says about this world (John 7:7; 1 John 2:16).
2. Contrast what the world exalts with what God exalts (Luke 16:15; 1 Cor. 1:26).
3. Fill your mind and heart with the word of God (Ps. 119:9).
4. Believe and acknowledge what God says about you in relation to the world (see verse three).

"For ye are dead." This declaration is stated as a matter of fact. Paul explains it in detail in Rom. 6-7. The Christian's flesh or old man is dead, and his new life as a Christian is actually **"hid with Christ in God."** This truth clarifies why a Christian can't lose his salvation: the eternal life that a Christian has is hidden with Christ inside of God! It can never be stolen from God!

The doctrinal explanation of verse three is explained back in Col. 2:12 where the believer's spirit is said to be baptized into Christ. This spiritual baptism, where the believer is buried "with him" (Col. 2:12 with Rom. 6:3, 4), perfectly matches **"hid with Christ."**

"Christ, who is our life." Notice that the new life of a Christian is synonymous with Christ Himself. Compare this with the following:

...even in his Son Jesus Christ. This is the true God, and eternal life. (1 John 5:20)

Jesus said unto her, I am the resurrection, and the life: he that believeth in me, though he were dead, yet shall he live. (John 11:25)

Jesus saith unto him, I am the way, the truth, and the life: no man cometh unto the Father, but by me. (John 14:6)

He that hath the Son hath life; and he that hath not the Son of God hath not life. (1 John 5:12)

In other words, Jesus Christ *is* our eternal life, for He *is* "the life" (John 14:6). This truth is the reason we tell unsaved people they must receive a person – the Lord Jesus Christ. They can't get eternal life without Him because He and eternal life are so closely connected that they are almost one and the same.

Practically speaking, verse four states for a Christian, Christ is everything – He *is* life itself. Life has no meaning outside of Jesus Christ, no purpose without the Lord. Neither is there any hope without Him. Look at Paul's statement concerning the resurrection of Christ:

If in this life only we have hope in Christ, we are of all men most miserable. (1 Cor. 15:19)

"Shall appear." Paul ties everything together in verses 1-4 by giving us the proper *up-look*. The word **"appear"** refers to the rapture (see Titus 2:13; 1 Peter 5:4; 1 John 2:28 and 3:2).

This is what he stated:

1. Your old life is dead, and you are risen with Christ to a new life.
2. Everything a Christian is, and everything he has is because of Christ and through Christ.
3. One day the Lord will appear to call you away to glory with Him.
4. Since all the above is literal and true it should affect how you live.
5. You should have your heart's desires and affections on the Lord and spiritual things instead of earthly carnal things.

Verses 1-4 are called practical theology. They deal with where "the rubber meets the road" in Christianity. Without a doubt, Jesus Christ is coming again. If you are saved, you will live with Him forever. He saved you from this wicked world, so you could live with Him in glory. Don't waste your life seeking treasures or carnal things "on the earth." Your old man is dead, so let him stay dead. Don't resurrect him. Let Christ live out His life in you to the glory of God.

Next, Paul goes on to tell us how to do this:

---

5 Mortify therefore your members which are upon the earth; fornication, uncleanness, inordinate affection, evil concupiscence, and covetousness, which is idolatry:

6 For which things' sake the wrath of God cometh on the children of disobedience:

7 In the which ye also walked some time, when ye lived in them.

The word **"mortify,"** of course, means to kill or destroy. Webster's 1828 dictionary also defines it as "to subdue or bring into subjection." There are *five* things that we are to "put to death" The following partial definitions are from that dictionary:

1. Fornication – sex outside of marriage boundaries

2. Uncleanness – moral impurity; dirtiness; filthiness

3. Inordinate affection – disorderly or excessive passion; not limited to rules; immoderate passion

4. Evil concupiscence – lust; unlawful desire of sexual pleasures

5. Covetousness – to covet with strong desire

"Covetousness, which is idolatry." Compare this with Eph. 5:5. While many Christians are not guilty of committing idolatry with graven images like Catholics, many are idolaters because of their covetous hearts. A man can have an idol in his heart even if he doesn't physically worship in front of a block of wood or stone:

> Son of man, these men have set up their idols in their heart, and put the stumblingblock of their iniquity before their face: should I be inquired of at all by them? Therefore speak unto them, and say unto them, Thus saith the Lord GOD; Every man of the house of Israel that setteth up his idols in his heart, and putteth the stumblingblock of his iniquity before his face, and cometh to the prophet; I the LORD will answer him that cometh according to the multitude of his idols; That I may take the house of Israel in their own heart, because they are all estranged from me through their idols. (Ezek. 14:3-5)

> For this ye know, that no whoremonger, nor unclean person, nor covetous man, who is an idolater, hath any inheritance in the kingdom of Christ and of God. (Eph. 5:5)

"For which things' sake." In other words: "The reason God's wrath is on the world is because of these wicked sins. **"Ye lived in them."** You used to do these things, but you shouldn't *now!*

The Bible is always clear on this point. A Christian should live differently than the unsaved world. God saved you out of the world to be a chosen vessel of purity unto Him! Even though we still have the presence of the old man with us, we should "put off" these deeds and follow Christ.

---

8 But now ye also put off all these; anger, wrath, malice, blasphemy, filthy communication out of your mouth.

9 Lie not one to another, seeing that ye have put off the old man with his deeds;

Paul uses the illustration of "putting off" and "putting on" in the manner you would change coats. As a new creature in Christ, you are to **"put off"** sins and "put on" righteousness. Although there is no spiritual checklist of *dos* and *don'ts* there are still some things every Christian should **"put off."** Six **"deeds"** are listed in verses 8-9.

1. Anger – Everyone experiences anger, and for the right reasons it is even allowed (see Eph. 4:26 and Mark 3:5). Anger for wrong reasons, however, belongs to the old man and needs to be **"put off."**

2. Wrath – Wrath is "violent anger" (Webster's 1828), the type of anger which leads to violence, revealing a genuinely uncontrolled temper.

3. Malice – Malice is defined by Webster as "extreme enmity of heart, or malevolence." Malice comes from an angry heart full of envy and hatred (Titus 3:3).

4. Blasphemy – A blasphemer speaks evil toward or about God (see 1 Kings 21:10, Ps. 74:18, Isa. 52:5). He may blame God for his circumstances and thus voice his blasphemy.

5. Filthy communication – Different from blasphemy and cursing, filthy communication would include things like vile or dirty talk, including jokes and innuendos.

6. Lying – No definition is needed for this. Not only should we refrain from falsehoods with our mouths, but we should also live a "truthful" life. We should be "above board" and honest in our dealings.

So, as a believer we are to **"put off the old man"** and **"put on the new man."** The old man is synonymous to the flesh or that part of the Christian that did *not* get born again. This old man is still corrupt and deceitful and will not be conformed to Christ until it is physically changed at the rapture. Note:

That ye put off concerning the former conversation the old man, which is corrupt according to the deceitful lusts. (Eph. 4:22)

That which is born of the flesh is flesh; and that which is born of the Spirit is spirit. (John 3:6)

For whom he did foreknow, he also did predestinate to be conformed to the image of his Son, that he might be the firstborn among many brethren. (Rom. 8:29)

For our conversation is in heaven; from whence also we look for the Saviour, the Lord Jesus Christ: Who shall change our vile body, that it may be fashioned like unto his glorious body, according to the working whereby he is able even to subdue all things unto himself. (Phil. 3:20-21)

As a Christian you will never be rid of the old man until it dies, or the Lord changes it at the rapture. Since it is not saved, it remains carnal, against God and His will for you. This doctrine (often called the two natures of the believer) explains why Christians still sin after salvation.

---

10 And have put on the new *man*, which is renewed in knowledge after the image of him that created him:

11 Where there is neither Greek nor Jew, circumcision nor uncircumcision, Barbarian, Scythian, bond *nor* free: but Christ *is* all, and in all.

Verse ten explains that one way to fight this old man is to **"put on the new man."** Romans 6-8 also gives insight for this battle.

Who is the new man? The new man is none other than the Lord Jesus Christ Himself who lives inside of every believer! Note:

The first man is of the earth, earthy: the second man is the Lord from heaven. (1 Cor. 15:47)

But put ye on the Lord Jesus Christ, and make not provision for the flesh, to fulfil the lusts thereof. (Rom. 13:14)

In verse ten, notice the connection between the new man and the **"image of him that created him."** The image is the Lord Jesus (see 2 Cor. 4:4 and Heb. 1:3) and the renewing can only come from the divine intervention of the Holy Spirit (Titus 3:5).

Doctrinally, the Christian has two sides to him: an old, wicked nature that is corrupt, after Adam and a new nature that is pure and holy which is actually "Christ in you, the hope of glory" (Col. 1:27).

This new man can dwell in the body of any individual, regardless of race, social status, or cultural background (verse eleven).

Practically, the text speaks of personal consecration and holiness. Christians should **"put off"** the old man and be renewed in mind and purpose by following the Lord Jesus Christ. The text states that we are to both **"put off"** the old man and also **"put on"** the Lord. In other words, you repent from wickedness by turning toward righteousness. You shouldn't stop some things without starting to do others. The quitting and beginning should go together.

---

12 Put on therefore, as the elect of God, holy and beloved, bowels of mercies, kindness, humbleness of mind, meekness, longsuffering;

13 Forbearing one another, and forgiving one another, if any man have a quarrel against any: even as Christ forgave you, so also *do* ye.

14 And above all these things *put on* charity, which is the bond of perfectness.

Because we are **"the elect of God, holy and beloved,"** Paul lists some things we are to **"put on"** so that Christians can act, talk, and live differently than the world. Paul says in Eph. 4:1 that we should "walk worthy of the vocation wherewith ye are called."

Here is the list:

1. Bowels of mercies – refer to the inner feelings of man. Our hearts should be filled with mercy, refraining from giving someone treatment he might deserve.

2. Kindness – of course, means to be kind. Unfortunately, we must be told to be kind because bestowing kindness might wound your pride or curb your selfishness.

3. Humbleness of mind – means applying the knowledge of the scriptures to produce a biblical estimation of ourselves. Humility will help us approach the Lord and other people with the right perspective.

4. Meekness – and weakness are not synonymous. Meekness is a personal choice while weakness is not. Jesus was meek (Matt. 11:29) but not weak. He was kind and gentle but also full of power. Meekness, kindness, and gentleness are all attributes of God (Ps. 117:2; 18:35) which He wants us to emulate.

5. Longsuffering – is the patient enduring of offense. It is the opposite of being hasty or quick to judge or condemn.

6. Forbearance – is one step up from longsuffering. It is the refraining from the enforcement of something that is due, such as a debt, right, or obligation.

7. Forgiveness – is probably the most understood yet least practiced term on the entire list. We are to have a forgiving spirit whether or not the offending party asks for forgiveness.

8. Charity – a word never found in the NIV or the New King James Version (NKJV), means more than just love. It is **"the bond of perfectness,"** implying some action or proof of love that we should demonstrate toward the brethren and a lost world.

15 And let the peace of God rule in your hearts, to the which also ye are called in one body; and be ye thankful.

16 Let the word of Christ dwell in you richly in all wisdom; teaching and admonishing one another in psalms and hymns and spiritual songs, singing with grace in your hearts to the Lord.

We are to **"let the peace of God rule"** in our hearts, leading us in every circumstance of life. Jesus promised to leave His peace with us:

Peace I leave with you, my peace I give unto you: not as the world giveth, give I unto you. Let not your heart be troubled, neither let it be afraid. (John 14:27)

Peace comes first with salvation by faith in the blood of Christ (Rom. 5:1, 9) and then after salvation by sincere, honest prayer (Phil. 4:6-7).

Our circumstances and "cares of this world" (Mark 4:19) shouldn't control our emotions, God's peace should! Think about it. If you are saved, you have Almighty God as your Father! He knows what you are going through, and He is with you no matter how hard it may seem. God is in control, and "we know that all things work together for good to them that love God, to them who are the called according to his purpose" (Rom. 8:28).

"Be ye thankful." Over and over the Bible repeats this message (1 Thess. 5:18). We are to have grateful hearts always. Thanklessness toward God reveals spiritual apathy and a need for repentance! The decline of a nation begins with ingratitude to God (see Rom. 1:21).

"Let the word of Christ dwell in you richly." includes the words of Christ on earth and the Bible itself. But a few things must first be true:

1. You must make room for the word in your heart (Matt. 13:15, 16).

2. You must listen to the word (Matt. 11:15).

3. You must read the word (Mark 12:10).

4. You must expose your heart to solid Bible preaching, which is the method God has chosen to "manifest his word" (Titus 1:3).

5. You must *obey* the word in order for it to dwell in you "**richly.**" Let it influence your personal life!

"Teaching and admonishing one another." We have lost the burden to mentor and disciple other people. Many Christians and church members simply leave this job up to the preacher as they do many other tasks. But Paul is not writing to the elders at Colosse but rather to the entire church! How are we to admonish one another?

1. Psalms – the collection of written songs in the Old Testament. Many of them have been set to music.

2. Hymns - the collection of accepted traditional Christian songs collated and passed down through the years.

3. Spiritual songs – any song that glorifies the Lord and edifies the hearer. These songs may be traditional (hymns), scripture (Psalms) or modern in their origin. [The fact that most Christians think modern "praise and worship" music is "spiritual" is a sign of the apostasy and carnality of today's church.]

---

17 And whatsoever ye do in word or deed, *do* all in the name of the Lord Jesus, giving thanks to God and the Father by him.

Verse seventeen sums up the entire Christian experience. No matter what you do (work, recreation, family, anything), you should be able to do it in the name of the Lord and give Him thanks. If your activity does not meet those qualifications, ask yourself whether or not you should be doing it.

Phillips (page 188) outlines the verse as:

Everything should be done *proportionately*: words *and* deeds.

Everything must be done *properly*: in the name of the Lord Jesus.

Everything must be done *prayerfully*: giving thanks.

---

18 Wives, submit yourselves unto your own husbands, as it is fit in the Lord.

19 Husbands, love *your* wives, and be not bitter against them.

20 Children, obey *your* parents in all things: for this is well pleasing unto the Lord.

21 Fathers, provoke not your children *to anger*, lest they be discouraged.

This last section of the chapter deals with God's plan for family and social order at home and at work. A concise summary is as follows:

1. Wives are to submit to their husbands.

2. Husbands are to love their wives.

3. Children are to obey their parents.

4. Fathers are not to provoke their children to anger.

5. Servants are to obey their masters.

6. Everyone is to do these things **"as to the Lord, and not unto men."**

God has set boundaries and guidelines for family and social order. Most marriages have problems because either the husband or wife will not follow his or her role as set forth in the Bible.

"Wives submit yourselves." The wife's role in marriage can be overlooked or even twisted. There are two common extremes. The first makes the wife a doormat to be ruled and eventually ruined by her husband. The second, the modern liberal approach, claims equality for each marriage partner. But God never said that husbands and wives were equal, nor did He give husbands blind leadership. He did, however, clarify their roles in the context. Below are some parallel passages relating to the wife's role:

> Wives, submit yourselves unto your own husbands, as unto the Lord. For the husband is the head of the wife, even as Christ is the head of the church: and he is the saviour of the body. Therefore as the church is subject unto Christ, so let the wives be to their own husbands in every thing. (Eph. 5:22-24)

> But I would have you know, that the head of every man is Christ; and the head of the woman is the man; and the head of Christ is God. (1 Cor. 11:4)

> But I suffer not a woman to teach, nor to usurp authority over the man, but to be in silence. For Adam was first formed, then Eve. (1 Tim. 2:12-13)

> Likewise, ye wives, be in subjection to your own husbands; that, if any obey not the word, they also may without the word be won by the conversation of the wives; While they behold your chaste conversation coupled with fear. Whose adorning let it not be that outward adorning of plaiting the hair, and of wearing of gold, or of putting on of apparel; But let it be the hidden man of the heart, in that which is not corruptible, even the ornament of a meek and quiet spirit, which is in the sight of God of great price. For after this manner in the old time the holy women also, who trusted in God, adorned themselves, being in subjection unto their own husbands: Even as Sara obeyed Abraham, calling him lord: whose daughters ye are, as long as ye do well, and are not afraid with any amazement. (1 Peter 3:1-6)

The text makes these things clear:

1. A wife is to submit to her own husband, not someone else's husband (Col. 3:18).

2. A wife's submission doesn't make her less of an individual. Submission is what she is to do, not who she is!

3. A wife is to submit **"as it is fit."** Some requests may not be "fitting" for a Christian woman. For example, no Christian wife must buy alcohol at her husband's request. The husband cannot *require* his wife to sin.

4. A wife should submit out of love (Eph. 5:23-24) because she knows her husband will die for her. She also submits because she recognizes the hierarchy that God has ordained (1 Cor. 11:4). If she wants God's blessing, she must follow God's program. Furthermore, she submits because God made her to be her husband's help meet. Adam was made first and then Eve was made for him, not the other way around (1 Tim. 2:12-13).

5. A wife is to submit **"in every thing"** (Eph. 5:24), not just when she chooses to. In other words, she is to please her husband, not herself.

6. A wife should understand how the Lord can use her obedience to God (1 Peter 3) in regard to dealing with a stubborn or unspiritual husband.

Whether you are a husband or a wife, you are to follow God's will for *your* role whether your partner does or not! You are not responsible for their actions toward you, only your actions toward them. At the end of the day, you will be the one giving account to the Lord, not your spouse!

"Husbands, love your wives." Although the Bible does tell wives to "love their husbands" (Titus 2:4), Phillips (192) is right that in this passage "the instructions for the wife are addressed to her will while the instructions to the husband are addressed to his heart."

The following are some corresponding passages dealing with the husband's role:

> But I would have you know, that the head of every man is Christ; and the head of the woman is the man; and the head of Christ is God. (1 Cor. 11:3)

> Husbands, love your wives, even as Christ also loved the church, and gave himself for it. (Eph. 5:25)

> So ought men to love their wives as their own bodies. He that loveth his wife loveth himself. For no man ever yet hated his own flesh; but nourisheth and cherisheth it, even as the Lord the church. (Eph. 5:28-29)

> Likewise, ye husbands, dwell with them according to knowledge, giving honour unto the wife, as unto the weaker vessel, and as being heirs together of the grace of life; that your prayers be not hindered. (1 Peter 3:7)

The highlighted points would be:

1. A husband is supposed to be in submission to the Lord Jesus Christ (1 Cor. 11:3). He should not expect his wife to submit to him if he himself will not submit to God.
2. A husband is to love his wife with the love that the Lord Jesus had for us – sacrificial love (Col. 3:19; Eph. 5:25).
3. A husband's love is nourishing (Eph. 5:29) to the wife. His love should build her up, not put her down.
4. This love is "cherishing" (Eph. 5:29) and caring.

5. This love has no bitterness (Col. 3:19) and is unconditional even if the wife does not submit in the biblical manner. The Christian husband should love her for who she is, not for what she can do to please him! Compare this to Christ's love!

6. A husband is to have knowledge about his wife (1 Peter 3:7). He should know her well enough to know what is best for her and the family. A husband is a caretaker of a vineyard!

7. A husband is to honor his wife (1 Peter 3:7). He is not to be-little her or treat her as a servant. He is to treat her as a beloved queen (see the Song of Solomon).

8. If a husband does not lead his wife and family, every aspect of their lives will be affected, including his own relationship with God (1 Peter 3:7).

Scripturally, the majority of the responsibility in a marriage is the husbands. He is to take the leadership position so that the wife doesn't have to. He is to take the leadership even if his wife is "contentious" (Prov. 21:19) because she can't have her way. The Bible clearly delineates the roles, and failure to heed to God's program will end in certain disaster.

"Children, obey your parents." Parents would do well to paste verse twenty on the refrigerator because today many think that the children have just as much "say so" as the parents. Just take a trip to the local fast-food restaurant and you will see this philosophy in action. The parent lets the two-year-old determine everything from what flavor soda to order to where he wants to sit! Soon the parents will be asking the children for financial advice! It's crazy! Children ruling over parents and women ruling over men are signs of spiritual apostasy:

And I will give children to be their princes, and babes shall rule over them. (Isa. 3:4)

As for my people, children are their oppressors, and women rule over them. O my people, they which lead thee cause thee to err, and destroy the way of thy paths. (Isa. 3:12)

Even though it may not be popular, children are still instructed by God to be submissive and obedient to their parents and specifically to their fathers (see verse twenty-one). There must be an established social structure if the child is to flourish according to God's program.

"This is well pleasing unto the Lord." Children need to understand that by obeying their parents, they are pleasing the Lord. Ephesians 6:2 complements this verse.

---

22 Servants, obey in all things *your* masters according to the flesh; not with eyeservice, as menpleasers; but in singleness of heart, fearing God:

23 And whatsoever ye do, do *it* heartily, as to the Lord, and not unto men;

24 Knowing that of the Lord ye shall receive the reward of the inheritance: for ye serve the Lord Christ.

25 But he that doeth wrong shall receive for the wrong which he hath done: and there is no respect of persons.

Verse twenty-two instructs about servants. Of course, in modern America slavery is not part of our social paradigm as it was in the first century. We can, however, learn some application for the workplace between employers and employees.

"Servants." Some people have a hard time with the biblical position regarding slavery in the Bible. In fact, some go as far to condemn the Bible because it makes allowance for the institution of slavery. Below are a few things for you to consider:

1. The Bible's allowance for this social institution doesn't mean that it condones any *perversion* or *evil* within this institution.

2. The Bible never condones the abuse of a slave.

3. Cultural considerations are necessary for understanding scriptural mandates in certain passages. In Paul's day, for instance, men kissed each other (Rom. 16:16), so there was a command regarding such. But just because God had to deal with things that were part of the social fabric of that day doesn't mean that He always thought them best for mankind. In fact, God also permitted polygamy, much like He did slavery.

4. While Christianity often reforms governments and social ills, it is not intended to change all social structure, at least not in this dispensation. When the Lord Jesus returns, then the spiritual and physical kingdoms will be united in harmony under Him. Until then, Christians are given guidelines (like here) how to act under these arrangements.

"Servants, obey in all things." Notice that Christian servants are not told to rebel or to attempt to escape their servitude. They are told to serve well because in doing so they are serving **"the Lord Christ"** (verse twenty-four). Notice Paul's comment under the inspiration of the Holy Ghost:

> Let every man abide in the same calling wherein he was called. Art thou called being a servant? care not for it: but if thou mayest be made free, use it rather. For he that is called in the Lord, being a servant, is the Lord's freeman: likewise also he that is called, being free, is Christ's servant. (1 Cor. 7:20-22)

"Not with eyeservice, as menpleasers." That is, a Christian servant (or employee for us today) is not to work just when the boss is watching. You are not to work just to please someone: you are to work hard even when the manager is not watching, even when you are not being evaluated. You are to work hard because you are working for Someone in a higher position – God Himself.

Verse twenty-three will help any employee to keep things in perspective, for you are to work, not just with your mind, but with your heart **("heartily")**. As a Christian you are not working just to feed your family or yourself: you are working for the Master. Your testimony both on and off the job are important to the Lord. God is the One who gave you the job and the ability to perform those duties. You must give your best effort and all glory to Him because He is the One you are working for.

"Receive the reward of the inheritance." What a blessing it must have been for Christian slaves to read this. They never received any kind of inheritance, but because they were now in the family of God as "sons" (1 John 3:1, 2), they could look forward to rewards for their labor.

At the end of the chapter, before Paul moves on to the Master's responsibilities in chapter four, an addendum seems to be tacked on: **"and there is no respect of persons."** Here is a reminder that God doesn't recognize man-made social classes. Rather He is looking for a Christian that will follow His guidelines in obedience. Followers can earn great rewards, but rebels can earn grave consequences (verse twenty-five). Many a social problem could be prevented or avoided if God's word was heeded.

COLOSSIANS CHAPTER 4

---

1 Masters, give unto *your* servants that which is just and equal; knowing that ye also have a Master in heaven.

Today, Paul's directive to Christian masters would be applied to employers or managers.

Giving that which is **"just and equal"** is not an uncommon concept in the New Testament:

> And in the same house remain, eating and drinking such things as they give: for the labourer is worthy of his hire. Go not from house to house. (Luke 10:7)

Paul reminds masters that they, too, are slaves that will give account to their own **"Master in heaven."** Every Christian is "bought with a price" (1 Cor. 6:20). This reminder helps the Christian master realize that he will give account of how he treats and manages those that are under him.

---

2 Continue in prayer, and watch in the same with thanksgiving;

In all of Paul's epistles, he repeatedly emphasizes that we should spend time in prayer and fellowship. When considering all the references, Paul is doing more than telling us to pray – he is telling us to *live* in prayer. Note:

> For this cause we also, since the day we heard it, do not cease to pray for you, and to desire that ye might be filled with the knowledge of his will in all wisdom and spiritual understanding. (Col. 1:9)

> Pray without ceasing. (1 Thess. 5:17)

> Wherefore also we pray always for you, that our God would count you worthy of this calling, and fulfil all the good pleasure of his goodness, and the work of faith with power. (2 Thess. 1:11)

> I will therefore that men pray every where, lifting up holy hands, without wrath and doubting. (1 Tim. 2:8)

> Rejoicing in hope; patient in tribulation; continuing instant in prayer. (Rom. 12:12)

> Defraud ye not one the other, except it be with consent for a time, that ye may give yourselves to fasting and prayer; and come together again, that Satan tempt you not for your incontinency. (1 Cor. 7:5)

> Ye also helping together by prayer for us, that for the gift bestowed upon us by the means of many persons thanks may be given by many on our behalf. (2 Cor. 1:11)

> Praying always with all prayer and supplication in the Spirit, and watching thereunto with all perseverance and supplication for all saints. (Eph. 6:18)

> Be careful for nothing; but in every thing by prayer and supplication with thanksgiving let your requests be made known unto God. (Phil. 4:6)

"Watch the same with thanksgiving." Just as Jesus told His disciples to "watch and pray" (Matt. 26:41), we, too, are to watch while we pray by being alert and observant. We are to recognize when God answers a prayer and then be thankful **("with thanksgiving")** with a grateful heart toward God. As much, if not more of our prayer time, should be spent thanking and glorifying the Lord rather than asking for things!

---

3 Withal praying also for us, that God would open unto us a door of utterance, to speak the mystery of Christ, for which I am also in bonds:

4 That I may make it manifest, as I ought to speak.

Paul never thought he was above asking for prayer nor hesitated to ask for it (see 1 Thess. 5:25; 2 Thess. 3:1; Heb. 13:18) because he knew that God answers prayer. Some Christians would get more help if they would simply ask others to pray for them. Specific details are not absolutely necessary although sometimes they may be helpful.

In this instance, Paul asked the Colossians to pray that the Lord would open a **"door of utterance,"** so they could preach the gospel. This verse, along with Acts 14:27; 1 Cor. 16:9, and 2 Cor. 12:2, is where the common expression "waiting for God to open a door" comes from. Unfortunately, many Christians are so eager to "do something for God" (what a paradox!) that they never wait for the Lord to open the door. Christians should pray that the Lord open a door of opportunity and then be prepared to go through it when He does.

The **"mystery of Christ"** refers to Col. 1:26, 27 and the mystery revealed to the apostle Paul about Christ indwelling the believer. This revelation explains why Paul called the gospel "*his* gospel" (Rom. 2:16; 16:25; 2 Tim. 2:8).

"That I may make it manifest." Since God gave us the Bible to reveal Himself, not to hide Himself, it is the preacher's job to make the scriptures **"manifest."** A clear, concise exegesis of the scriptures is what is needed today:

So they read in the book in the law of God distinctly, and gave the sense, and caused them to understand the reading. (Neh. 8:8)

Today, expertise in preaching the Bible has nearly disappeared. Instead of *expounding* the scriptures to make them manifest, preachers *use* the scriptures to teach and preach their own agendas. Some preachers regurgitate the convictions or opinions of another preacher. While others preach *issues,* simply saying whatever comes to their mind while preaching. They may both *use* some Bible verses to justify their positions, but the sermons themselves are not structured around the Bible. Sermons should be built around the scripture instead of the other way around.

"As I ought to speak." Paul knew how his ministry and preaching **"ought"** to be, and he strove to meet that level of excellence. But he also knew that he could not do it alone – God had to open the right doors. Paul was dependent on God to work, so he could be faithful in carrying out his orders.

---

5 Walk in wisdom toward them that are without, redeeming the time.

Christians are to be wise in dealing with the **lost ("them that are without").** How you act in the unsaved world could mean everlasting life or eternal death for those who see you! Your behavior should always point others to Christ rather than away from Him. Anything less is a bad testimony. Paul deals with some of these matters in 1 Cor. 10:27-33.

"Redeeming the time." No one can go back and retrieve time. It is non-renewable. But we are to use our time wisely because time is precious in view of eternity. The Bible exudes a sense of urgency, a sense of imminence regarding the Lord's return and our short lives. James said that life was "even a vapour, that appeareth for a little time" (James 4:14). A few other verses that emphasize this truth are listed below:

Redeeming the time, because the days are evil. (Eph. 5:16)

And that, knowing the time, that now it is high time to awake out of sleep: for now is our salvation nearer than when we believed. The night is far spent, the day is at hand: let us therefore cast off the works of darkness, and let us put on the armour of light. (Rom. 13:11-12)

---

6 Let your speech *be* alway with grace, seasoned with salt, that ye may know how ye ought to answer every man.

Since people communicate primarily by speech, a Christian needs to be sure that his speech conforms to Bible standards. If your heart is right, your speech will also be right.

Jesus said, "[O]ut of the abundance of the heart the mouth speaketh" (Matt. 12:34). If you clean up your speech only to please those around you or to "play the part," you will be a Pharisee. But the Lord declares that the heart determines a person's words (Deut. 6:5). If your heart is right, what you say will please the Lord.

Being "slow to speak" (James 1:19) is a valuable strategy. Instead of blurting out whatever comes to mind, *think* before you speak!

In the multitude of words there wanteth not sin: but he that refraineth his lips is wise. (Prov. 10:19)

Whenever a Christian speaks, whether in preaching or in private conversation, his speech should be according to the word of God:

If any man speak, let him speak as the oracles of God. (1 Peter 4:11)

Much of the foolish conversation and "jesting" (Eph. 5:4) that one hears is completely out of line and has little or no value whatsoever.

"Let your speech be alway with grace." Notice the word **"alway"** is used here like it is in Philippians 4:4. It has two meanings:

1. In every kind of way
2. At all times

"With grace." Grace is the opposite of judgment or wrath. Grace is God *not* giving us what we deserve. Since we were initially saved by grace (Eph. 2:8, 9), we are also to stand by grace (Rom. 5:2). We are to let grace rule us (Rom. 5:21). We should not "frustrate the grace of God" (Gal. 2:21). A great way to live in this marvelous grace is to let our speech be covered in grace. The Lord Jesus Himself spoke "gracious words" (Luke 4:22), and we should follow His example.

Some insist that our speech should have more condemnation than grace. But condemning speech is always easier than gracious speech. And condemnation has a greater tendency to be carnal. But when we must reprove or correct, we should do so with the right spirit and attitude, and never with condescension or hateful vindictiveness.

> Brethren, if a man be overtaken in a fault, ye which are spiritual, restore such an one in the spirit of meekness; considering thyself, lest thou also be tempted. (Gal. 6:1)

"Seasoned with salt." In the context, salt has to do with witnessing or apologetics **("answer every man"),** and it is the next component of good Christian conversation.

And though we should have grace and compassion when dealing with people, we also should use a little "salt." Jesus said that we are the "salt of the earth" (Matt. 5:13). Phillips (pages 207-208) points out that:

> Salt does three things: It adds tang. Many foods would be tasteless were it not for salt....[Salt] arrests corruption...and salt creates thirst.

One reason the world is not drawn to Christ, or our churches is because there is no "tang" to our lives. Instead of our speech creating a thirst in the unbeliever, we are tasteless and bland. Even gracious speech needs salt to flavor the conversation. And too much grace can turn into lasciviousness (Jude 4). Christians are supposed to relate what the Bible says; even if it seems 'unsavory' (e.g., all have sinned). In fact, unsavory truths are often necessary in a conversation. But though the Christian speaks with salt, he should still speak with compassion.

Distinct types of salt are used for various situations:

1. Rock salt is used on the streets for quick immediate reaction.
2. Table salt is used at the dinner table to add taste.
3. Saline solution is salt diluted in water used to aid healing.

It would be foolish to employ the use of rock salt at a dinner table. Likewise, to use saline solution on streets covered with ice is equally foolish. When using "salt," discretion and wisdom are a must.

"That ye may know how ye ought to answer every man." In this chapter Paul has been refuting the errors of the Gnostics (the "knowers"). And here he is telling the Colossians that though they do need knowledge of the Bible, they don't need the knowledge of the world. The Bible can always answer a world that has no clue. When you consider it, the unsaved world has no idea

1. Where they came from.

2. What they are doing here.

3. Where they are headed.

The Bible, however, answers these three problems and many more. And the Christian should know enough of the word to answer "and to convince the gainsayers" (Titus 1:9):

> But sanctify the Lord God in your hearts: and be ready always to give an answer to every man that asketh you a reason of the hope that is in you with meekness and fear. (1 Peter 3:15)

I'm not suggesting that every Christian should be a theological scholar. But the Bible teaches that Christians should know what they believe and why they believe it in order to share their beliefs with others.

In the final ten verses, Paul mentions some friends of the ministry. Phillips (210) has outlined these men as

1. Tychicus: the faithful man.

2. Onesimus: the fugitive man.

3. Aristarchus: the fearless man.

4. Marcus: the forgiven man.

5. Justus: the friendly man.

6. Epaphras: the fervent man.

7. Luke: the famous man.

8. Demas: the floundering man.

9. Nymphas: the fruitful man.

10. Archippus: the faltering man.

11. Paul: the fettered man.

Wiersbe (150-152) has classified these men as

1. The men who stayed (Aristarchus, John Mark, Jesus Justus, Luke).
2. The man who prayed (Epaphras).
3. The man who strayed (Demas).

---

7 All my state shall Tychicus declare unto you, *who is* a beloved brother, and a faithful minister and fellowservant in the Lord:

8 Whom I have sent unto you for the same purpose, that he might know your estate, and comfort your hearts;

In Acts 20:4, Tychicus is mentioned as a companion with Paul on his third missionary journey. He is also mentioned again in Eph. 6:20; 2 Tim. 4:12, and Titus 3:12. Tychicus is the one who delivered this epistle, the epistle to the Ephesians, and possibly the epistle to Philemon.

Paul had assigned Tychicus four tasks:

1. Deliver this epistle.
2. Tell them how Paul was doing.
3. Find out how they were doing.
4. Comfort them.

---

9 With Onesimus, a faithful and beloved brother, who is *one* of you. They shall make known unto you all things which *are done* here.

Onesimus was a runaway slave who was probably from the city of Colosse (**"who is one of you"**). Paul sent him and Tychicus together.

10 Aristarchus my fellowprisoner saluteth you, and Marcus, sister's son to Barnabas, (touching whom ye received commandments: if he come unto you, receive him;)

11 And Jesus, which is called Justus, who are of the circumcision. These only *are my* fellowworkers unto the kingdom of God, which have been a comfort unto me.

Aristarchus was from Thessalonica (Acts 20:4) and had accompanied Paul on his third journey. They had gone to Ephesus and were also shipwrecked on the way to Rome (Acts 27:2). He was a **"fellowprisoner"** with Paul, with both suffering in jail for Christ. "Tradition has it that he was martyred by Nero" (Phillips, 216). Whether or not that was the case, Paul considered him a close and valuable friend in the ministry. He knew what Paul was experiencing because he went through it too.

John Mark is mentioned next, **("Marcus, sister's son to Barnabas")** included as one of the Hebrews **("who are of the circumcision")** that was with Paul.

Paul had forgiven him for his departure when he and Barnabas were in Perga (Acts 13:13). At the end of Paul's life, Paul stated that "Mark" was "profitable to me for the ministry." (2 Tim. 4:11).

"Touching whom ye received commandments: if he come unto you, receive him." Whether this has to do with the gospel of Mark is unclear. His gospel may have already been in circulation at this time.

"And Jesus, which is called Justus." The name *Jesus* was a common name – the Hebrew equivalent is Joshua. Hence you will find Moses' successor Joshua called Jesus in Acts 7:45 and Heb. 4:8. There is also another man named Bar-jesus (literally "the son of Jesus") mentioned in Acts 13:6.

Mark and Justus are said to be **"fellowworkers"** and a **"comfort"** to Paul.

12 Epaphras, who is *one* of you, a servant of Christ, saluteth you, always labouring fervently for you in prayers, that ye may stand perfect and complete in all the will of God.

13 For I bear him record, that he hath a great zeal for you, and them *that are* in Laodicea, and them in Hierapolis.

Epaphras seems to have been the pastor or at least *a* pastor of the church at Colosse. Note:

> As ye also learned of Epaphras our dear fellowservant, who is for you a faithful minister of Christ. (Col. 1:7)

He is called their minister and was included as one of them **("one of you").**

"Always labouring fervently for you in prayers." Epaphras regarded the spiritual condition of the Colossians seriously, spending time and effort praying for them. No doubt this epistle was at least in part an answer from God.

Epaphras prayed that every aspect of their lives would be conformed to the **"will of God,"** including their doctrine. He prayed not for his will for them, but rather that they would learn to please God! What concern and love he had for this flock.

Epaphras also had zeal, love, and concern for the churches in Laodicea and Hierapolis (see verse thirteen) both of which were close to the church at Colosse.

14 Luke, the beloved physician, and Demas, greet you.

Although Luke's name occurs only two times in the entire New Testament – here and in 2 Tim. 2:11 – his influence and blessing to the apostle Paul and Christianity is immeasurable. Luke was very much **"beloved."**

He seems to have joined Paul in Acts 16:10 before Paul went to Philippi. And since the apostolic gifts would soon cease (notice Paul's comment in 2 Tim. 4:20 and 1 Tim. 5:23) Paul would need a physician to help him deal with his many infirmities and "thorns."

Luke was also a very astute historian, chronicling the life of Jesus Christ. And, who better than a medical doctor to record the record of the virgin birth? His gospel is the longest gospel account (and the longest book of the New Testament). Later, Luke authored the book of Acts – the history of the early church, which would light the fires of evangelism for centuries to come.

Since Luke was mentioned in this list and not said to be **"of the circumcision,"** scholars have assumed that both Luke and Demas were Gentiles instead of Jews. If that were the case, then Luke would be the only Gentile author of scripture. Below are some reasons that support Luke being a Jew:

1. Since the "oracles of God" were given to the Jews (Rom. 3:2) reason follows that every author of the Bible would be Jewish. The early church was completely Jewish, as were all the disciples and our Lord.

2. Luke had a vast personal knowledge of Jewish customs and ceremonies (see Luke 1).

3. If Luke were a Gentile, why weren't the Jews accusing him, instead of Trophimus, of defiling the temple in Acts 21?

"And Demas, greet you." Paul doesn't say much about Demas. Was he already beginning to wander away from the Lord? We can only guess. Later, Paul writes that Demas left him, "having loved this present world" (2 Tim. 4:10).

---

15 Salute the brethren which are in Laodicea, and Nymphas, and the church which is in his house.

16 And when this epistle is read among you, cause that it be read also in the church of the Laodiceans; and that ye likewise read the *epistle* from Laodicea.

Paul sends a greeting to Nymphas because the church at Laodicea was in his house, and Paul had instructed the Colossians to pass this letter on to that church. **"Church which is in his house"** is not an uncommon occurrence in the New Testament (see Rom. 16:5 and Philem. 24). In fact, churches mostly assembled in houses. Did you know that there are no church buildings mentioned in the New Testament? Christians first met from "house to house" (Acts 2:46; 20:20; 1 Tim. 5:13) because the various churches were in houses (not that there is anything wrong with church buildings.)

When people use the word *church* today, they are usually referring to a building or structure. But in the New Testament "church" does not mean a structure. Rather it means a group of people, whether corporately as the entire body of Christ (Eph. 1:22, 23) or locally as an individual assembly (Acts 11:22).

"Read the epistle from Laodicea." Paul sends this letter to the Colossians telling them to trade epistles with Laodicea, so both congregations can read both epistles. So where is this letter Paul wrote to the Laodiceans? We do not know. Although some scholars assume it is the epistle to the Ephesians, the Bible does not support the idea. Ephesians 1:1 says, "to the saints which are at Ephesus."

Unfortunately, people worry about the books they don't have while ignoring the ones they have. This instance also shows the importance of preservation. You see, there are some books that God *inspired* but did not choose to *preserve*. God's omissions are equally as important as His additions.

Other unpreserved books mentioned but not included in scripture are:

1. The book of the wars of the Lord (Num. 21:14).
2. The book of Jasher (Josh. 10:13; 2 Sam. 1:18).
3. The book of the acts of Solomon (1 Kings 11:41).
4. The book of the Chronicles of the Kings of Israel (1 Kings 15:31).
5. The book of Samuel the Seer (1 Chron. 29:29).
6. The book of Nathan the prophet (1 Chron. 29:29; 2 Chron. 9:29).
7. The book of Gad the Seer (1 Chron. 29:29).
8. The book of Shemaiah (2 Chron. 12:15).
9. The book of Jehu (2 Chron. 20:34).
10. The book of the records (Ezra 4:15).
11. The prophecy of Ahijah the Shilonite and visions of Iddo the seer (2 Chron. 29:29).
12. The story of the book of the Kings (2 Chron. 24:27).

---

17 And say to Archippus, Take heed to the ministry which thou hast received in the Lord, that thou fulfil it.

Archippus may have been kin to Philemon (see Philem. 2). At any rate, Paul is sending a lay person to encourage the preacher because sometimes even preachers need encouragement!

Maybe Archippus didn't value the ministry as much as he should, being concerned with other things. And while the ministry is a very taxing life, all ministers must remember that their calling is holy, and God expects them to be faithful to their duties.

"Received in the Lord." This phrase testifies that the ministry is a calling not a career. The world has convinced the church that pastors are only hirelings who work for their pay. Nothing could be further from the truth. A church should offer monetary support as a gift to the minister. And, if possible, the minister should seek to live by the gospel:

> Even so hath the Lord ordained that they which preach the gospel should live of the gospel. (1 Cor. 9:14)

"Fulfil it" is just Paul telling Archippus to do the job God has called him to do. Our Lord finished His work, and we should do the same:

> I have glorified thee on the earth: I have finished the work which thou gavest me to do. (John 17:4)

---

18 The salutation by the hand of me Paul. Remember my bonds. Grace be with you. Amen.

Although Paul didn't physically write the letter (he dictated it), he did sign it, as he did most of his epistles. The postscript (which is found in some Bibles) says, "Written from Rome to the Colossians by Tychicus and Onesimus."

"Remember my bonds." Paul is reminding them of his prayer in verses 3, 4. He wants to be released, so he can preach the gospel. One can almost hear Heb. 13:3 along with this verse:

> Remember them that are in bonds, as bound with them; and them which suffer adversity, as being yourselves also in the body. (Heb. 13:3)

PHILEMON

INTRODUCTION

The book of Philemon was written by the apostle Paul around the same time as Colossians and Ephesians (approximately AD 60-64). He wrote this third shortest book in the Bible (only 430 words – Vance, 218) while in prison at Rome.

As McGee (496) notes, "There were approximately sixty million slaves in the Roman Empire where the total population did not exceed one hundred twenty million." This short letter concerns one of those sixty million slaves in the little town of Colosse. This small city would never be discussed in modern times had not these letters from Paul been written. You see, Colosse was destroyed completely by an earthquake about two years after Paul's letters were delivered (Phillips, 15).

The story behind this very personal letter is intriguing. A slave, named Onesimus had escaped from his master Philemon – a wealthy member of the church at Colosse. But while in Rome Onesimus had been led to the Lord by Paul while he was in prison (verse ten). Whether or not Onesimus set out to find Paul in hopes that he might aid him in returning to his old master (Baugh, 514) or was simply providentially guided to Paul is not clear.

What is clear however, is that Onesimus was a "new creature" in Christ (2 Cor. 5:17) and wanted to do the right and lawful thing of the day – return to his master, and Paul wrote this letter to Philemon to assist Onesimus in this task. And as we shall see, Paul does much more for Onesimus than simply asking Philemon to receive him back as a slave (see verses 15, 16).

It is also interesting that according to the postscript, Onesimus wrote this letter at the hand of Paul. He and Tychicus would deliver the epistle to the Colossians together (Col. 4:7-9) and then Onesimus would go on alone to the house of Philemon.

Doctrinally the book illustrates the great truth of imputation (verse eighteen); that Jesus Christ has taken the sins that were on our account and given us His righteousness that was on His account!

Practically it teaches "brotherly love" (McGee, 498) and forgiveness; that "if any man be in Christ, he is a new creature" (2 Cor. 5:17) and we are to accept them as such.

Politically, it teaches that Christians are not to merge church and state affairs together. Paul never tried to overthrow the social institution of slavery, nor did he champion political issues. Instead, he preached the "unsearchable riches of Christ" (Eph. 3:8). Note Alexander Maclaren's remarks (cited by Wiersbe, 272) regarding Christianity's role in society and politics.

First, the message of Christianity is primarily to individuals, and only secondarily to society. It leaves the units whom it has influenced to influence the mass. Second, it acts on spiritual and moral sentiment, and only afterwards and consequently on deeds or institutions. Third, it hates violence, and trusts wholly to enlightened conscience. So it meddles directly with no political or social arrangements, but lays down principles which will profoundly affect these, and leaves them to soak into the general mind.

PHILEMON CHAPTER 1

---

1 Paul, a prisoner of Jesus Christ, and Timothy *our* brother, unto Philemon our dearly beloved, and fellowlabourer,

2 And to *our* beloved Apphia, and Archippus our fellowsoldier, and to the church in thy house:

3 Grace to you, and peace, from God our Father and the Lord Jesus Christ.

"Paul, a prisoner of Jesus Christ." Notice in this greeting that Paul does not use the title "apostle." I believe he does this on purpose because, as we shall see, he identifies himself with the slave Onesimus (verse seventeen). Slaves of that day were pretty much prisoners. They couldn't come and go when they wanted. They had to do what their master's wanted. In other places Paul calls himself a "servant" (Rom. 1:1; Gal. 1:10; Titus 1:1).

"And Timothy our brother." Timothy is with Paul, as were Epaphras, Marcus, Aristarchus, Demas and Luke (verses 23-24). As Dr. Ruckman notes (185) this is Paul's first imprisonment, where he was on "house arrest." In other words, he could receive visitors and still have somewhat of an outreach (see Acts 28:30).

"Unto Philemon our dearly beloved, and fellowlabourer." As we stated, Philemon was a wealthy man in the church at Colosse. Since there is no record of Paul ever visiting Colosse, we infer that Philemon was converted during the Ephesus campaign of Acts 19. Paul considers him a close Christian friend and comrade. He wasn't just a Christian in word, but also in deed **("fellowlabourer").**

"Beloved Apphia, and Archippus." Because of the personal nature of this letter, it seems likely that Apphia was the wife of Philemon and Archippus his son. Archippus was mentioned in the letter to the Colossians regarding the ministry (Col. 4:17). So, maybe he was pastoring this small church that was meeting in Philemon's house.

"Church in thy house." In the day of modern construction and American tradition, it is hard for us to think of a church without of the actual building that houses the church. But the truth of the matter is that the church itself is *not* the physical structure at all! The church is composed of people. Years ago, people referred to the church building as the meeting house, or the place where the church assembled. The word "church" is used two ways in scripture:

1. The local assembly (which could be composed of saved *and* lost people).

> And when this epistle is read among you, cause that it be read also in the church of the Laodiceans; and that ye likewise read the epistle from Laodicea. (Col. 4:16)

2. All born again people.

> And hath put all things under his feet, and gave him to be the head over all things to the church, Which is his body, the fulness of him that filleth all in all. (Eph. 1:22-23)

Great edifices were *not* the norm for the early church. They met in homes or wherever they could meet. The people, for the most part, were poor. When the church (as a whole) finally gained a position of financial means (in the Laodicean age – Rev. 3:17), it succumbed to the idea that nice buildings and grounds, along with large numbers were signs of spirituality. This great error was fostered long ago by the corrupt Roman Catholic Church and her children, and even further back by the northern tribes of Israel. We forget that you can lose God in a "building program."

For Israel hath forgotten his Maker, and buildeth temples…(Hos. 8:14)

Verse three verifies again that this letter is more than a personal letter from one friend to another. It **is "from God our Father and our Lord Jesus Christ."**

---

4 I thank my God, making mention of thee always in my prayers,

5 Hearing of thy love and faith, which thou hast toward the Lord Jesus, and toward all saints;

6 That the communication of thy faith may become effectual by the acknowledging of every good thing which is in you in Christ Jesus.

7 For we have great joy and consolation in thy love, because the bowels of the saints are refreshed by thee, brother.

Paul's manner was one of thankfulness and prayer (verse four). He thanked God for Philemon and prayed for him. He had heard of Philemon's **"love and faith."** This "love" for God was evident in Philemon's life because it was shown not only toward the Lord but to others **("toward all saints.")** Here we stumble upon a great truth concerning our walk with God. If we are to love God the right way, we must love the brethren the right way. The two are linked. And as Phillips states (244) "love is what makes faith evident [and]…faith is what makes our new life in Christ effective."

"The communication of thy faith." You see, it's not enough for you to have faith if you are not exercising it and spreading it. You might have faith, but it will not be **"effectual."** It will not do anything. It will simply be dormant.

---

8 Wherefore, though I might be much bold in Christ to enjoin thee that which is convenient,

9 Yet for love's sake I rather beseech *thee*, being such an one as Paul the aged, and now also a prisoner of Jesus Christ.

Paul is saying that he could be **"bold in Christ"** and demand this request of Philemon, but he won't. He's not going to use his apostolic authority to guilt trip Philemon into doing anything. And as Phillips notes (250):

> A person can be made to follow a given line of behavior from one of three reasons…discipline, out of a sense of duty, or out of a sense of desire. Discipline says, 'I have to'; duty says, 'I ought to'; desire says, 'I want to.'

"Yet for love's sake." Paul is asking out of love and expects Philemon's obedience out of love.

Notice also that he is asking as one that is not in a position of authority or rule. He is asking as **"Paul the aged…and prisoner of Jesus Christ."**

"Paul the aged." The scriptures have a lot to say about age, both young and old. While the normal life span allotted is seventy (Ps. 90:10), there is no age limit for serving God. There might be a maturity level (1 Tim. 3:6) but not an age level.

---

10 I beseech thee for my son Onesimus, whom I have begotten in my bonds:

11 Which in time past was to thee unprofitable, but now profitable to thee and to me:

Paul finally gets to what this letter is about. Of course, we can assume that Philemon had some idea since Onesimus was the one who handed it to him. Oh, how scared Onesimus must have been! The contrast between Onesimus and Uriah is obvious. Both carried letters with them – one for his freedom and the other for his death (2 Sam. 11:15).

"Begotten in my bonds." In other words, Paul has led him to saving faith in the Lord Jesus Christ. Onesimus as **"begotten"** or "born again" (John 3:3-5). It means that Paul was his "spiritual father" in the faith, but of course, there is no record that his converts ever called him "father."

And last of all he was seen of me also, as of one born out of due time. (1 Cor. 15:8)

For though ye have ten thousand instructors in Christ, yet have ye not many fathers: for in Christ Jesus I have begotten you through the gospel. (1 Cor. 4:15)

My little children, of whom I travail in birth again until Christ be formed in you. (Gal. 4:19)

Unto Timothy, my own son in the faith: Grace, mercy, and peace, from God our Father and Jesus Christ our Lord. (1 Tim. 1:2)

To Titus, mine own son after the common faith: Grace, mercy, and peace, from God the Father and the Lord Jesus Christ our Saviour. (Titus 1:4)

"Which in time past was to thee unprofitable." Onesimus, which means "profitable," was a runaway slave. He probably even stole from Philemon in order to survive on his journey to Rome (see verse eighteen). But, as Paul writes, Onesimus is a changed man! He is now a Christian. He has been with Paul for some time now, and Paul vouches for his character and even says that he is **"profitable to thee and to me."** What a difference Jesus Christ can make in a person's life!

12 Whom I have sent again: thou therefore receive him, that is, mine own bowels:

13 Whom I would have retained with me, that in thy stead he might have ministered unto me in the bonds of the gospel:

Verse twelve seems to indicate that the idea of Onesimus going back was conceived by Paul **("whom I have sent")**. But at any rate, Onesimus went back. He didn't run or flee, or we never would have this epistle.

"Receive him, that is, mine own bowels." The word "bowels" is used in the sense of the heart (see 2 Cor. 6:12; Phil. 1:8; Col. 3:12; 1 John 3:17). Paul is hinting at the substitution he will mention more clearly in verse seventeen.

"Whom I would have retained with me." Paul, even though he was imprisoned, evidently had the liberty to request the service of Onesimus if he so desired. Onesimus must have been a great help to the aged apostle and prisoner. He is saying that he could have just asked Onesimus to stay and serve Paul in the place of Philemon, because Philemon was so far away.

14 But without thy mind would I do nothing; that thy benefit should not be as it were of necessity, but willingly.

But, if he kept Onesimus, it wouldn't really be like Philemon was helping Paul since Philemon wouldn't have willingly sent Onesimus there. Again, the best service is out of desire, not duty or discipline.

15 For perhaps he therefore departed for a season, that thou shouldest receive him for ever;

16 Not now as a servant, but above a servant, a brother beloved, specially to me, but how much more unto thee, both in the flesh, and in the Lord?

Onesimus did leave Philemon. He was wrong and broke the law, which, if Philemon was not a good Christian, he could have Onesimus tortured and possibly killed.

"Receive him for ever." In other words, Paul is saying that your fellowship with him is to be restored and there will be no need for you to get rid of him or ever part from him.

"Not now as a servant." While Paul had already given instruction on the proper treatment of slaves (see Col. 4:1; Eph. 6:9), here he is expecting Philemon to treat Onesimus different from a mere slave. He was to treat him as **"a brother beloved."** This seems to indicate that Paul was implying that Onesimus be freed, which was not an easy or cheap thing to do (Acts 22:28). Verse seventeen verifies this:

---

17 If thou count me therefore a partner, receive him as myself.

"Receive him as myself." If Philemon was to receive Onesimus in place of Paul, surely he wouldn't have Paul become his slave! Paul is urging Philemon to treat Onesimus as he would if Paul were set free from prison and a guest in his house.

In typology we can certainly apply this to salvation. We *were* the servants of sin, but now we are set free in Christ (John 8:34; Rom. 6:17). We are **"accepted in the beloved"** (Eph. 1:6). God has received us and will welcome us into heaven just as if we were His only begotten Son!

---

18 If he hath wronged thee, or oweth *thee* ought, put that on mine account;

19 I Paul have written *it* with mine own hand, I will repay *it*: albeit I do not say to thee how thou owest unto me even thine own self besides.

Paul is aware that Onesimus probably stole from Philemon in order to run away. How else would a slave have the financial means to make a journey from Colosse to Rome? He is telling Philemon to simply forgive Onesimus (Matt. 18:27).

"Put that on mine account." He adds this in case Philemon has a problem forgiving Onesimus. Paul pushes the reasoning of substitution to the limit. He is assuming all responsibility for Onesimus, including any debts he might have. He then goes on to verify that he is good to his word **("I will repay it.")**.

"Thou owest unto me even thing own self besides." But then he reminds Philemon of what he owes Paul. He uses some leverage in this matter. The least Philemon could do is what Paul is asking. After all, had it not been for the apostle Paul, Philemon would still be lost and on his way to hell.

These verses illustrate the great doctrines of *Imputation* and *Substitution*. Substitution teaches that Christ took our place, and Imputation comes from the word "impute" which means "to attribute," to "charge." Imputation teaches that believers are given Christ's righteousness. We were the "servants of sin" (Rom. 6:17, 20), but Jesus Christ died in our place (Substitution). Since Jesus died in our place, our sins were put on His account. In exchange the sinner who trusts Jesus' death for his salvation is *freely* given the righteousness of Christ – a clear sinless record! He took our sins and gave us His righteousness!

> But for us also, to whom it shall be imputed, if we believe on him that raised up Jesus our Lord from the dead; Who was delivered for our offences, and was raised again for our justification. (Rom 4:24-25)

The sinner who believes is guaranteed this great salvation because Jesus rose from the dead! We *know* His promise is true because He is alive and He verified this transaction by appearing in the presence of God for us, where God declared us to be innocent and free from the guilt and punishment of sin – that's "justification."

---

20 Yea, brother, let me have joy of thee in the Lord: refresh my bowels in the Lord.

21 Having confidence in thy obedience I wrote unto thee, knowing that thou wilt also do more than I say.

Paul had **"confidence"** that Philemon would receive Onesimus and follow his "orders." And knowing that Philemon would do this (and even more) brought Paul **"joy"** and **"refresh[ing]."**

---

22 But withal prepare me also a lodging: for I trust that through your prayers I shall be given unto you.

Paul still had hopes of getting out and visiting Philemon, as he did the Philippians (Phil. 1:25). The anticipated arrival of Paul no doubt would be a great incentive for both Philemon and Onesimus to carry out Paul's wishes (Phillips, 263).

This verse also indicates that Paul was imprisoned twice, not once. The first imprisonment would be Acts 28 and the second 2 Timothy 4. During the first imprisonment he would have access to visitors and friends (as Timothy here) – see Acts 28:23, while the second imprisonment Demas was gone (2 Tim. 4:10) Mark was restored (2 Tim. 4:11) and Trophimus was left at Miletum sick (2 Tim. 4:20). None of these fit his imprisonment in Acts 28.

Did Paul ever get out and go see Philemon? Well, there is never any indication (in 2 Timothy or elsewhere) that he did. There is a hint that he wanted to go into Spain (Rom. 15:24, 28). And as Dr. Ruckman (215) notes:

> If Paul followed through on the plans that he made before he went to Jerusalem, then when he was released from his first imprisonment, he didn't go back *east* to Asia Minor. He traveled *west* to Spain…And from the character of early Celtic Christianity in England, there is a possibility that Paul may have gone on to the British Isles before returning to Rome on his way back to Colosse…

---

23 There salute thee Epaphras, my fellowprisoner in Christ Jesus;

24 Marcus, Aristarchus, Demas, Lucas, my fellowlabourers.

25 The grace of our Lord Jesus Christ *be* with your spirit. Amen.

As we said, these men are not mentioned as being with him during the imprisonment in 2 Timothy 4.

"Epaphras, my fellowprisoner." Epaphras, as you recall was the pastor of the church at Colosse. He now found himself in Paul's situation as a fellow prisoner.

"Marcus, Aristarchus, Demas, Lucas." He calls all four of these men his **"fellowlabourers."** Mark wrote the gospel of Mark. Aristarchus is mentioned in Acts 19:29; 20:4; 27:2 and Col. 4:10. He was a Macedonian and a fellow prisoner. Demas of course would later leave and go back into the world (2 Tim. 4:10). And Luke was Paul's great friend and medical missionary (Col. 4:10). He authored both Luke and the book of Acts.

"The grace of our Lord Jesus Christ be with your spirit. Amen." He concludes this short letter with a word from our Lord. And that word is **"grace."** What a fitting word to end this captivating letter of freedom and love.

BIBLIOGRAPHY

American Dictionary of the English Language. https://webstersdictionary 1828.com/.

Baugh, Steven M. "Philemon" In *Zondervan Illustrated Bible Backgrounds Commentary*. Vol. 3, *Romans to Philemon*. Edited by Clinton E. Arnold, 513-19. Grand Rapids: Zondervan, 2002.

Chafer, Lewis Sperry. *Systematic Theology*. Vols 1 & 2. Grand Rapids: Kregel, 1976.

Cloud, David W. *Way of Life Encyclopedia of the Bible & Christianity*. 4th ed. Port Huron, MI: Way of Life Literature, 2002.

Ironside, H. A. *Philippians and Colossians*. Grand Rapids: Kregel, 2007.

McGee, J. Vernon. *Thru the Bible with J. Vernon McGee*. Vol. 5, *1 Corinthians-Revelation*. Pasadena: Thru the Bible Radio, 1983.

Merriam-Webster Dictionary. https://www.merriam-webster.com/.

Phillips, John. *Exploring Colossians & Philemon: An Expository Commentary*. Grand Rapids: Kregel, 2002.

————. *Exploring Ephesians & Philippians: An Expository Commentary*. Grand Rapids: Kregel, 1993, 1995

Random House College Dictionary. New York: Random House, 1973.

Ravenhill, Leonard. *Why Revival Tarries*. Bloomington, MN: Bethany House, 1950, 1987.

Ruckman, Peter S. *How To Teach Dispensational Truth*. Pensacola: Bible Baptist Bookstore, 1992.

———. *The Books of 1 & 2 Thessalonians and Philemon*. Pensacola: Bible Baptist Bookstore, 2005.

———. *The Books of Galatians, Ephesians, Philippians, Colossians*. Pensacola: Bible Baptist Bookstore, 1973.

———. *The Christian's Handbook of Science and Philosophy*. Pensacola: Bible Baptist Bookstore, 1985.

Schaff, Philip. *History of the Christian Church*. Vol. 4. Peabody, MA: Hendrickson, 1885, 2006.

Tozer, A. W. *The Knowledge of the Holy*. New York: HarperCollins, 1961.

Vance, Laurence M. *King James, His Bible, and Its Translators*. 3rd ed. Pensacola: Vance Publications, 2022.

Walker, David E., *The Bible Believer's Guide to Dispensationalism*. 2ND ed. Miamitown OH: Daystar, 2006.

Wiersbe, Warren W. *The Bible Exposition Commentary: New Testament*. Vol. 2. Colorado Springs: Cook Communications Ministries, 2001.

Printed in Great Britain
by Amazon

62937038R00107